THE PARENT'S SECTION:
OUTSIDE THE LOCKER ROOM

SIMONE JOYE

THE PARENT'S SECTION: OUTSIDE THE LOCKER ROOM

Copyright © 2022 by S Joye & Associates LLC

All rights are reserved. No part of this book may be replicated or transmitted in any form or by any means, electronic or mechanical, including photocopying without permission from the Author.

LIMIT OF LIABILITY/DISCLAIMER OF WARRANTY
The resources available in this book and eBook are for informational purposes only and not for providing legal or medical advice of any kind.

The opinions expressed are the opinions of the individual author.

The Publisher and the Author make no representations or warranties with respect to the accuracy or completeness of the contents of this work and expressly disclaim all warranties. No warranty may be created or extended by sales or promotional materials. Furthermore, the author occasionally uses terms and phrases that may suggest she offers direct and actionable advice. In such cases, the author is not to be received as advisement of any kind. Access to this book and eBook does not create an advisory relationship of any kind with its reader.

For information about special discounts for bulk purchases and media inquiries, please contact S Joye & Associates at ceo@simonejoye.com or 301-725-1572.
Website: simonejoye.com.

FIRST EDITION

ISBN: 978-0-9995276-8-9   (Hardcover)
ISBN: 978-0-9995276-7-2   (Paperback)
ISBN: 978-0-9995276-6-5   (eBook)

Front Cover Design: Dylan Johnson
Back Cover Photo courtesy of David Cordova
Printed in the United States of America

S Joye & Associates LLC
5422 Ebenezer Road, Unit 444
White Marsh, MD 21162

CONTENTS

Dedication VI
Acknowledgments VII
Introduction IX

Chapter I PARENTS: THE REAL MVPs 1
   Do You Have the Fortitude? 6
   Your Time Will Not Be Your Own 7
   Circumventing The Parent's Role 9
   Financial Costs to Expect 11
   Rewards Parents Can Be Thankful For 16
   Dream Chaser 20
   Parents as a Positive Influence 23
   Team Parents 35

Chapter II COACHES & PARENTS WORKING TOGETHER ... 41
   High School Coaches 42
   Grassroots and AAU Coaches 43
   College Coaches 45
   The Power of Coaches 47
   Collaborating with Coaches 48
   Trust the Process | It's Just Business 50
   Final Thoughts on Coaches 54
   Referees/Officials 57

Chapter III THE EARLY YEARS & HIGH SCHOOL..................59
- The Early Years..................59
- High School Years..................60
- Academics as a Priority..................61
- Grade by Grade..................63
- The High School Difference: Public vs. Private Schools..........65
- Catholic, Christian, and Prep High Schools..................66
- Basketball Academies: Another High School Option..............69
- Reclassification..................72
- Post-Graduate Year..................74
- National High School Basketball Tournaments..................74
- High School Basketball Fun Facts..................75

Chapter IV THE OTHER SEASONS: GRASSROOTS & AAU ... 77
- Sponsored vs. Non-Sponsored Teams..................81
- Basketball Camps..................88
- Taking It to The Street(Ball)..................90
- Personal Training and Personal Coaches..................91

Chapter V COLLEGE RECRUITMENT & SCHOLARSHIPS..... 95
- What is a Basketball Scholarship?..................97
- Governing Associations for College Athletics..................99
- College Basketball Conferences..................100
- College Division Levels – Finding the Right Fit..................102
- Historically Black Colleges and Universities (HBCUs)..........103
- Junior College (JUCOs)..................107
- Basketball Ratings and Rankings..................108
- Preparing for Recruitment..................110
- Visits During the Evaluation Process..................119
- Selecting a College..................124
- No Scholarship Offer? It is Not Over...................128

Chapter VI HEALTH & WELLNESS..................131
- Physical Health..................132
- 5 Health Priorities Parents Should Monitor..................135
- Mental Health Wellness: *"They Forget We Are Kids."*..........143
- Pain Management and Medication..................149
- Harmful Drug Usage: Marijuana and Fentanyl..................150
- Nutritional Health..................151
- Sexual and Other Abuse in Sports..................153

Chapter VII BRANDING & MAKING MONEY 157
   Name, Image, and Likeness (NIL) 157
   NIL Opportunities and Support 160
   Online Exposure and Social Media.. 161
   Highlight Videos, Photos, and Media Interviews 162

Chapter VIII GOING PRO 165
   Sports Agents.. 167
   Professional Leagues.. 169
   How Do Prospects Enter the NBA?... 170
   Playing Overseas and Worldwide Governing Body................ 174
   Other Professional Teams and Leagues 175
   Final Thoughts on Going Pro.. 177

Chapter IX BASKETBALL HISTORY & RESOURCES 179
   Noteworthy Contributors to Young People in Basketball... 180
   Other Notable People and Places in Men's Basketball 185
   Basketball Associations and Advocacy 187
   Basketball Informational Websites 189
   Twitter Accounts Parents May Find Interesting..................... 191
   Basketball Films, TV Shows & Documentaries 193
   Basketball Books.. 197
   Basketball Podcasts 198

Author's Video Conclusion 199
About the Author 200
Beyond the Book with Simone Joye 201
In Memory Of 202
References... 203

DEDICATION

God first. Always. Thank you for my blessings.

To the **basketball parents**:
The road is complex and congested.
Remember, behind every child who believes in themselves,
there is a parent who believes first.
May this book be an invaluable asset in your basketball journey!

To my number 1 daughter, ***A'Shey Venning***:
You're priceless! There are no words to describe how much I love and appreciate you!

To my number 1 son, ***Chad Venning***:
I am so proud of you. Never forget #NoOneStopsTheDream.
Trust the journey. Love you!

To my father, ***Roney Eford, Sr.*** (1941-1977)
You left us too soon.
Your earthly gifts and talent still transcend time.
I know you watch over us. Gone but never forgotten.
Until we meet again. Rest in Peace.

*In Memory of "**Coach Al**" **Eford, Jr.***
(1955-2022)

ACKNOWLEDGMENTS

Coach Jacque Rivera—Thank you for helping to clear the way. You are a phenomenal coach and parent supporter! #ForeverFamily

Coach Julius Allen—When they look up the word coach in the dictionary, there you are! Thank you for helping Chad. You're truly a gem!

St. Bonaventure University—"There is no knowledge without love." To the entire coaching staff, athletic director, and administration—thank you, #32 is off to a great start! #GoBonnies!

Coach Kevin Broadus, Morgan State—You put Chad on a national stage—twice—thank you.

Coach Brian Merritt—Thank you for helping Chad more than you had to.

Coach Ken Hoyte, Ph.D.—Thank you for Chad's first college tour when he was not even on your team. Keep showing young people what is possible.

Reverend Edward Allen, Philemon Baptist Church (Newark, NJ)—We are forever grateful for your prayers, love and mentorship.

Ronn Taylor—God gave you the gift of prose. Thank you for being my editorial guru and friend for over 30 years!

Leah Wilcox—With a career-high of almost 40 years, you are one of the nation's most dynamic women in sports. You do not take any credit, but your tenure and grace inspire me.

Rod Strickland—For answering the phone for us on the gloomiest days, and for not letting stardom stop you from helping generations after you.

La Shone Adams—Thank you basketball mom! I appreciate your friendship.

Allyson M. Wynn—Thank you for sharing! You're an exciting and supportive basketball mom to Will Thomas (#Say10). Keep going!

INTRODUCTION

No thief, however skillful, can rob one of knowledge and that is why knowledge is the best and safest treasure to acquire."

— L. Frank Baum

In the United States, youth athletics is a $19 billion industry. Compare that to the operating budgets of the NFL ($17 billion) or the NBA ($10 billion), and you will understand why coaches often refer to it as "a business." Parents must remember to work inside the business or risk their student-athlete being pushed aside.

Many young people hope their basketball skills will garner a free college education and/or propel them to a professional career in the NBA, overseas, or in a new league. Rising in basketball is complex, and the road is congested. Traveling through can often be confusing, overwhelming, and glorious. How do parents and players get through it?

The Parent's Section: Outside The Locker Room is a guide for basketball parents who want to ensure their student-athlete has a fair shot at success. This book also provides an opportunity for coaches, and others near and dear to our children, to learn about parents' perspectives. Contrary to popular belief, parents can be an asset to coaches and basketball organizations.

Although this book can serve as a resource for all parents of athletes, my framework comes primarily from the boys/mens basketball world. This is the area I have been the most involved in. This does not negate the journey for girls/women who play basketball—I was one of them myself long ago, but there are vast differences.

For brevity, I refer to almost all higher education institutions as colleges. This book is not a personal journey, although personal references are warranted to share lived experiences. I appreciate my son, Chad Venning, for allowing me to share his.

Many parents can likely pinpoint when they first entered youth basketball. For me, it began when Chad decided to obtain a college basketball scholarship so I would not have to pay for him to attend college. That warmed my heart.

In the 8th grade, his father, a barber, and a friend (who also played basketball) convinced him that his then 6'5" frame would be better suited in boxing and on a basketball court.

For years, my plan was for Chad to grow up and attend Morehouse College. I was told he was likely the youngest to ever take an admissions tour at the age of four. A framed Morehouse T-shirt was gifted to him, and it adorned his bedroom wall for years. Chad would then graduate and work in law enforcement with the FBI or Secret Service. He loved robotics in elementary school, so I felt a NASA career could be on the horizon. Those were mommy's dreams.

Little did I know when basketball entered the foray that our lives would change at such a phenomenal speed. Or the arduous work it took as a divorced parent. It has been filled with family sacrifices, emotional rollercoasters, and hard work for my son, both on and off the court.

Years ago, when few gave him hope that he could be a great basketball player, I began secretly thinking of how to convince him to choose another career path. Then God blessed me with the opportunity to share an evening with Shaquille O'Neal's phenomenal mother, Lucille O'Neal. Our conversation inspired me to write this book. I went home and made a poster: *No One Stops The Dream*. Chad replaced the Morehouse T-shirt and set our family on *his* course.

That dream materialized when he signed his first Division 1 (D1) scholarship document.

"When you've been blessed, pass it on."[1]

It became clear that other basketball parents would likely appreciate help and encouragement. Youth sports should be about fun and wonderful experiences for young people. It has become a dream killer for too many of them. It is causing some of them to consider and commit suicide. Parents must also carefully maneuver through an ambiguous process to help their children succeed.

James Naismith, who created basketball *for* young people, only needed two sheets of paper to define "the rules." Yet the chance for an abundance of financial rewards, which Naismith did not participate in, has warped youth basketball and the true intent.

Parents must trust their own process and ensure their student-athlete is not lost in the process of others.

From one basketball parent to another...

Here is your blueprint.

CHILDREN UNDER
18 MUST BE
ACCOMPANIED
BY A PARENT OR
LEGAL GUARDIAN

#TEAM PARENTS

CHAPTER I

Parents: The Real MVPs

"We were not supposed to be here; You made us believe. You kept us off the street, put clothes on our backs, food on the table. When you didn't eat you made sure we ate. You went to sleep hungry. You sacrificed for us. You [Wanda Durant] are the real MVP."

— Kevin Durant

Young athletes are not just born; their parents raise them. Parents are usually their first coaches, with some creating basketball stars in their backyard. We are the drivers, the secretaries, the organizers, the tutors, the cheerleaders, the psychologists, and the influencers. Our vehicles adorn sports decals.

We share their accolades on our social media. We have excellent attendance at games, where we are squeezed together with other parents and spectators in crowded gyms. Some of us even bring our chairs. We cheer the loudest and stand in hallways and courtside long after others have left. You may also catch us in the parking lot, trying to catch a nap or killing time. We may also be at that 24-hour gym as our son works out. We may be at the physical therapy session where we are praying them back to good health. We ensure our kids are safe, have enough to eat, and have a comfortable and safe home. Most of all, as parents of athletes, we love them through wins, losses, injuries, and broken promises as they live out their sports dreams. We do not seek any credit, nor do we want the limelight. Most of us support our kids, ensure their happiness, and watch basketball.

It is irrefutable that the most successful players are those with actively involved parents. So why do many parents struggle through the youth basketball world? Why are parents' voices and suggestions missing from public conversations, panel discussions, and regulatory commissions?

Parents could also use help for our ability to engage with one another away from the gym. There is so much we can help one another with to benefit our student-athlete.

With all the changing rules and regulations, unwavering competition, and limited spots, trusting the process is not enough. The amount of information you can find about basketball is endless. Everyone who covers it appears to be an expert. One does not need a license to create a youth basketball program. No one regulates youth basketball, like in college basketball or the pros. It feels like a "get in where you fit in" industry. Mothers play a significant role in weeding their sons through. If baseball and football are sports for fathers and sons, basketball is the sport for mothers and sons. Have you ever wondered why many NBA players emotionally, and publicly, thank their mothers?

LeBron James told his mother after winning his fourth NBA Finals MVP award in 2020,

> *"Everything that you had been through, everything that I had seen, there's nothing that can stop me. I hope I continue to make you proud, Mom."*[2]

It is beautiful when sons give their acknowledgments. Mothers profoundly influence a student-athlete's basketball success. However, it appears that a basketball mom is just a by-product of our children, and we are regulated to the parent's section.

If you are a basketball mom like me, we are not sure anyone knows our first name. We are the "Mom of [name of player]." If we are divorced mothers, who use our maiden name, we are likely addressed by our son's last name. We do not bother correcting anyone—because they probably will not remember. On the contrary, in this male-dominated industry, fathers are always formally addressed with "Mr." in front of their name, or by their first name.

The time parents put in is crucial, and dare I state, moms do the most! You must have the stamina for early days and late nights that may exhaust you. Travel schedules and communications from coaches, trainers, teachers, and potential handlers will be consistent. You may never have a free weekend. As a mom, or dad, you must be all in or out. Ask yourself, "Am I up to the task?"

Going Home

The choice to relocate back home, from Georgia to New York City while Chad played in high school, was decided for me. My son wanted his divorced parents in the same city where he got his serious basketball start. Chad also needed a new high school because his father and I could not agree on what was more important, basketball or his education. His father wanted him to play with one of the top youth basketball coaches in New York City. My issue was that he worked in a school with poor graduation rates in a community plagued with gangs and violence.

One week before the start of the school year, I contacted Ed Gonzalez, the head basketball coach at Brooklyn's Bishop Loughlin High School.

Loughlin has a long history of producing great basketball players, including former NBA player Devin Ebanks (Saudi Premier League), Khadeen Carrington (Hapoel Jerusalem), Keith Williams (Otago Nuggets), Mike Boynton (the head basketball coach at Oklahoma State), and Mark Jackson, an ESPN commentator who played at St. John's before joining the New York Knicks. Twin brothers Justin Champaigne (Toronto Raptors) and Julian Champaigne (Philadelphia 76ers/Delaware Blue Coats), who were Chad's teammates, are recent graduates. It was there I met some great basketball parents.

Justin and Julian's parents were determined they would succeed and their sacrifices showed. Their father, Ranford, worked at Loughlin to help cover their tuition. Their mother, Christina, an elementary school teacher, was always an encouraging team parent to other moms. Another team parent, LaShone Adams, whose son Jaheim Young (Western Connecticut), showed up and out for other parents and the players. One year she hosted a beautiful dinner for the team at her home. LaShone and Christina showed me how to be an involved team parent and how we should care for all players, not just our own. They made the start of Chad's high school basketball journey easier for me because they cared.

Brooklyn was a special time. One minute I was spending my 10th anniversary in my beautiful suburban Georgia home, and in the blink of an eye, we were living in a 2-bedroom apartment in the East New York section of Brooklyn. Our cousin rented us an apartment she used for storage and our entire living room was full of furniture and boxes. We were cramped into a space barely the size of my former bedroom suite. When my daughter first visited, she could not understand how I appeared so comfortable with our new living arrangement.

"A mother does what she has to do," I told her.

My job was also over. I stepped down from serving as the executive director of Young People Matter (YPM). It was a nonprofit I had founded eight years earlier. I had spent almost a decade providing emergency shelter and helping homeless, runaways, and sexually exploited minors in Atlanta. My team and I had worked tirelessly to help over 4,000 young people and their families with funding support from the government, foundations, corporations and even media mogul Tyler Perry. I ran for the Georgia Assembly one year to bring awareness. I know I would have likely won my second campaign. The decision to leave all that behind was tough. Yet, although I miss Atlanta and helping young people directly, my son and daughter had to come first. I have no regrets.

Gonzalez and the school's administration accepted Chad, and although they provided a generous financial aid package, I only had a few days to pay $5,000 for his tuition.

My daughter decided to leave college in Maryland to finish in New York City to help with what we called, at the time, "basketball logistics." She also shared, "I'm back to make sure basketball doesn't kill my mother." We then moved into a three-bedroom apartment in the Midwood section of Brooklyn, and a New York City Councilmember gave me a job as his Communications Director. Chad started playing basketball at Loughlin, and our family became #TeamLoughlinLions.

The following spring, Chad joined the New York Gauchos, an AAU team in the Bronx, where he would take the subway three times a week after school. At 8 pm, I would leave our apartment to pick him up. We would return home at about 10:30 pm, and then it was time for dinner, homework, and preparation for the next day. In between, there were one-on-one lessons, academic support, and taking him to any available court to play daily. After the Gauchos, Chad played for Team Rio in central New Jersey. Another long commute from his school and our home in Brooklyn. This is a suitable time to add that coaches (pre-COVID) had never cancelled one of my son's practices. I used to dream about a day (or night) off. It could have been 11 degrees below zero, or thunderous rain pouring, and Chad would still have practice.

Three years later, something I had not predicted happened. Chad, once again, showed me how profound basketball was to him when he *left us* in Brooklyn for The MacDuffie School in Massachusetts. At MacDuffie his basketball IQ went to a higher level, and he decided basketball would be his future career beyond college. Although he got a late start in basketball, there was no turning back.

It took me six years and three more apartment rentals before deciding on a location to purchase and settle into another house. My story may be unique, but it is plausible to believe that basketball parents make serious and significant life changes. Some even send their pre-teen children to America from around the world and do not see them (in person) for years. Now *that* probably would have killed me.

> *"I think that moms can get an idea of what it means to kind of put yourself on the back burner and to help your kids pursue their dreams. It takes a lot of money and time and energy AND you have to really believe in and support your kids...That we take away from our own personal lives when we're in the gyms and practices and driving them here and there and flying to different cities for tournaments."*[3]

Nikki Burnett, mother of Nimari Burnett (University of Alabama)

Do You Have the Fortitude?

Being a basketball parent takes work and endurance. If you are going to start on this road, or are already there, being prepared is vital. You have to brace yourself and be ready for any adjustments.

The first time Chad had a game on Mother's Day, I was livid. Mainly because one thing I can count on from my kids is a fabulous Mother's Day from beginning to end. I learned that playing basketball on Mother's Day is a regular occurrence in youth basketball. Has any coach ever polled a mother to ask whether it is okay to schedule games on our sacred day? Coaches must have their own mothers they want to see. You would assume they may have a wife, who may be a mother, who deserves a day of pampering.

Not only are there games on Mother's Day, but tournaments as well. They also have inviting names, such as the Mother's Day Classics and the Mother's Day Weekend Invitational. That Mother's Day, I was thankful that at least my kids and I were together. My daughter pouted the whole ride. Any attempts to get her excited on that sunny day were futile.

Upon arrival, Chad's coach gave us a job when we walked into the fully packed multi-level facility with teams from around the tri-state area. "Mom, please keep score," he said as he pointed to a table. My daughter and I looked at each other in awe and thought he was joking. Chad gave us the look of "please do not embarrass me" before disappearing into a sea of players. We rolled up our sleeves and got to work. That day, I learned that you will be expected to contribute as a parent. You may be asked to keep score, be a referee, contact other parents, help with travel arrangements, give players a ride, or serve as a chaperone.

Another test was when Chad and our cousin, Al Eford, Jr., convinced me, as I suffered with the flu, to leave my bed to get Chad to an AAU "try-out" an hour away that he could not miss. When I arrived, I found Chad had been asked, along with some older players, to "scout" up-and-coming players for the team. There was no try-out. With tissues and cold medicine in my purse, I could not help but think, "Why me?"

One winter, against all sound advice from friends, I drove from New York City to Massachusetts for four hours through a storm. I look back at the video I made from my car (just in case) in wonderment at my bravery. However, I was willing to be a "super mom" because I could not let Chad be alone at his last game of the season or to travel home alone.

Basketball moms (siblings and dads) do it all. We miss family events and holidays, just like our sons. The online meme played out my life, "I can't [attend]. My son has a practice, game, or something."

Your Time Will Not Be Your Own

Off the court, there are no time boundaries. Youth basketball is a seven-day-a-week grind. At the last minute, a coach may call and ask your son to play—locally, or out of town. Do you have plans for school breaks? Yes, they have practice. Would you like to go on a family vacation? Find another date because they have a team meeting and practice. Even on Thanksgiving, your son may have a game. Does your son need a ride? Let the coach know as soon as possible, and they will find a way. Coaches are experts in moving players around, even at the last minute. Team absences are frowned upon. Players only get excused if there is a death or a mental health crisis. Even with an injury, they are expected to sit on the bench—crutches and all. More than one absence? You can believe the coach is already prepping for their replacement.

The term "student-athlete" was created by the NCAA as a legal strategy when the widow of
Ray Dennison
sought benefits after he died due to a head injury while playing college football. The Colorado Supreme Court declared the college was "not in the football business" and denied the claim.
Case: State Compensation Ins. Fund v. Industrial (1957)

Setting priorities for your child with schoolwork is also essential. The word "student" comes before "athlete" for a reason. Sometimes, your son will be tired or even exhausted, but that schoolwork will need to be completed. Teachers probably will not give them any leeway. Late-night games and practices will not be a viable excuse for missing class or school assignments. You may be up late with a cup of coffee, knowing you have your job the next day. Yet, there you are quizzing your son, washing uniforms, or helping him search for matching socks. Mom? Dad? Are you still up for this?

Basketball Moms

"The mother occupies a much more encouraging role and gives unconditional support; this support takes the form of emotional assistance, regardless of her child's actual sport performances, and is a result of the strong mother–child bond, which exists from early childhood."[4]

Research has proven that a basketball mom's engagement is unconditional. Yet, we hear the whispers, and we may get tested on our loyalty. Soccer moms can compete intensely for their children, who can also possibly make millions in the future, but basketball moms are judged when we do.

The media continues to purport us as the "single, low-income mother from the projects" stereotype. Lee Jenkins, a former senior writer at *Sports Illustrated*, gave his perspective on NBA mothers in his 2015 article, *Mom Look at Me Now*.

Although it was an overall great editorial, Jenkins states,

> *"They got pregnant and, despite challenges, carried to term. In many cases, they raised the boy alone, left to explain why fathers were absent."*

In a *New York Times* article, *NBA Zip Codes Matter*, author Seth-Stephens-Davidowitz reports,

> *"NBA players are 30 percent less likely to be born to an unmarried mother and a teenage mother."*[5]

Basketball moms of today are likely working women who are trying to manage it all.

THE PARENT'S SECTION: OUTSIDE THE LOCKER ROOM

Basketball Dads

If you're a basketball dad, many will be surprised to learn you exist, or have a relationship with your son. One day, Chad and I conversed with a coach who inquired about Chad's great performance at a game. Chad casually mentioned it was the game his grandfather attended for the first time. The coach, seemingly shocked, asked, "You know your grandfather?" He followed up with, "Are you close to your dad?" I was surprised at the questions. However, I would like to believe he meant no harm.

Yes, there are some deadbeat basketball fathers, like the character of Michael Rhodes, Sr., in *Tyler Perry's Meet the Browns*. Yet, I think it is essential to share that plenty of fathers, and grandfathers, committed to their next generation's success. Some are quiet influencers—others are more public. Perhaps the most famous is LaVar Ball, father of three NBA players, and the co-founder and CEO of their Big Baller Brand.

Tee Morant, the father of Ja Morant (Memphis Grizzles), recently wore a T-shirt to his son's game with the words "PROUD SUPPORTIVE DAD."

As evidenced by social media comments, many people were in a tizzy.

After all the backlash and commentary, Mr. Morant noted,

> *"They're not used to seeing a dad that's this in tune to the game and the fans and everything that is surrounded by pro basketball. So, I wore it like, 'Yo, this is what I stand for right here.'*[6]

At the 2022 NBA draft, 28 of the 30 first-round picks attended with their mother *and* father.

Circumventing The Parent's Role

Most young basketball players want to make a living playing the sport they love. They have no interest in becoming a celebrity, public figure, or even a role model for other kids. Adults are the ones who create that narrative. It also seeks to divide and conquer the parenting role. It begins in high school and on the AAU stages. Once a young basketball player gets attention and looks like there is potential to go far in basketball, the dynamic may shift.

Imagine the day a young man learns of anyone who only gave love and attention because they saw him as a meal ticket, in particular his own parents. There is no way the mental and emotional turmoil is worth it, even if they have the potential to become wealthy from their sports endeavors. Parents should not let the pursuit of money deny them the proper parenting bond with your child. Children are not property.

Patti LaBelle, in her book *Patti's Pearls* shares,

> *"There are some things you can't put a price on. Things like your dignity, your values, your self-worth and respect. They should never—not ever—be for sale, I don't care how stupid the money is."*

She also notes,

> *"I'm not saying that the benefits of professional success aren't real and rewarding. They are. But they won't make you happy, they won't sustain you, as you will find out the first time you sit down to eat Christmas dinner alone or you need to go to the emergency room in the middle of the night."*

Parents who replace love with financial gain of their basketball prodigies should be aware that there are stories of child actors and other celebrities, including Rihanna, who have sued their parents for overstepping in their success. The late Kobe Bryant sued a firm his parents hired because they were attempting to sell his high school memorabilia.[7] There are other stories of professional players who were once homeless, in the foster care system, or had parents who appeared out of the abyss feeling entitled to any newfound wealth basketball may afford them.

You should also be aware, and share with your son, that all the attention will vanish if they are counted out of basketball play for any reason. Will you still be there for him? Will his family? Will his coaches? His friends? It will be enough that there will be other adults ready to insert themselves into your child's life with ulterior motives. As a parent, you must use discernment with them, as well reporters, photographers, coaches, handlers, young girls (and women!), and negative family members.

A basketball parent's job is to ensure your son enjoys his childhood, completes his education, and has a healthy body and mind. It is also our job to raise great citizens who will positively contribute to society. For me, I want to believe it is working. It surprised and teared me up when I read Chad's words in his first newspaper interview, where he discussed YPM:

> *"Hopefully, one of these days, I can start that backup. Doing things from the kindness of your heart, that's what you should do. I always watched my mom do things for other people and wanted to do the same thing."*[8]

Financial Costs to Expect

> *"The most competitive teams vie for talent and travel to national tournaments. Others are elite in name only, siphoning expensive participation fees from parents of kids with little hope of making the high school varsity, let alone the pros.*[9]
> —Sean Gregory

The system is designed for parents to overspend on their student-athlete. John Engh, executive director of the National Alliance of Youth Sports, says parents of athletes "will spend at least 10% of their income on registration fees, travel, camps, and equipment."

It is easy to be sucked in because you are a parent and want your child to be happy. It may be difficult to share with your child that you cannot afford something—especially in basketball.

It was reported in an August 2017 *Time* cover story on the billion-dollar youth athletic industry:

> *"As expensive travel teams replace community leagues, more kids are getting shut out of organized sports. Some 41% of children from households earning $100,000 or more have participated in team sports. In households with income of $25,000 or less, participation is 19%."*[10]

Apply for a Youth Sports Grant

Every Kid Sports Pass is a youth grant to help cover sports registration fees for children 4-18 years old.

Parents can apply at everykidsports.org

Partners: Dick's Sporting Goods Foundation, Under Armour, Gatorade, NFL Flag, Snap!Raise and the Philadelphia 76ers.

Many young people are being left behind in sports due to the expenses and the dwindling lack of options in public schools and community centers.

One issue with paying for youth basketball activities is that parents are pressured to make fast payments. Therefore, even if it is affordable, budgeting is challenging. There is always something to pay for, no oversight, and you are lucky if you can get a receipt. Parents sometimes have no choice but to decline because the rent, or mortgage, is due. Will a coach or team owner work with you? Only if they need your son. If he is just an option, they will be on to the next parent, who will pay "today."

The following is a list of possible youth basketball expenses for parents to consider and ways to save money.

Private tuition and other school fees

If your son is playing basketball for any school, never pay 100% in tuition or fees. The school will likely offer financial assistance, and you should always negotiate. If they offer a 50% discount, ask for 60% if it helps. If you have a 529 College Savings Plan, the IRS allows you to use up to $10,000 for K-12 education costs.[11] Also, if your son attends school away from home, remember to budget transportation costs for them to travel to and from home several times a year.

Personal Trainers & Personal Coaches

These are costs for player development away from structured team activities. You may find a trainer, or coach, who may offer their services for free. You can offer to pay their facility rental costs. Depending on the rental costs, if they book several student-athletes on the same day, that could pay for the facility and provide a fee to them.

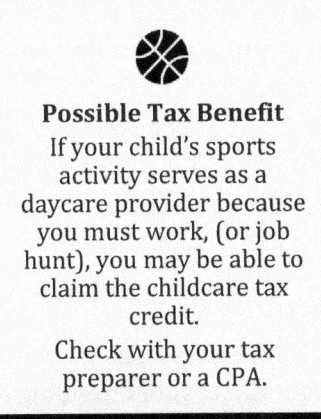

Possible Tax Benefit
If your child's sports activity serves as a daycare provider because you must work, (or job hunt), you may be able to claim the childcare tax credit.
Check with your tax preparer or a CPA.

Camp Registrations

There is no shortage of basketball camps, also known as "exposure" camps. Although they are advertised as seemingly once-in-a-lifetime opportunities for "top players," we learned the priority is profits over players. Parents can easily find themselves out hundreds of dollars. Do your research and ensure they can benefit your son. For example, will they make a highlight video? Will college coaches be in attendance? Is the facility licensed? Is the staff reputable?

As part of the college recruiting process, colleges also sponsor legitimate basketball camps.

If a college invites your son to a camp and is serious about his recruitment, they will not charge a fee. If a college camp has a fee, it may be worth it if your son is interested. The camp may provide an unbiased, candid evaluation of your son for his college recruitment. Registration fees average $100-$125. Your son may also have a chance to spend the night on campus, and you both may make great contacts. Several NBA players host (or sponsor) legitimate camps, including Kyrie Irving/Dallas Mavericks (2 days $249), Stephen Curry/Golden State Warriors (4 days: $695), and Udonis Haslem/Miami Heat (2 days: $169).

Coach Morgan Wootten (1931-2020) was the most well-known coach in high school basketball. He was the founder of a basketball camp in Virginia. On their website, it is referred to as "The World's #1 Instructional Basketball Camp." The camp, which has been operating since 1961, provides day and overnight camps for young people 7-16 years old. You can find more information at coachwootten.com. If you find free reputable camps in your area, and your son's schedule is free, take advantage.

Entrance Fees

Youth basketball games are not free to enter. Parents often complain about the cost of attending AAU, grassroots games, and other privately-run tournaments. The owners can set any price they like. Daily and weekend passes can easily cost $40-$100 per person versus a high school game ticket, usually $10-$15. I drew the line at having to pay when I had to "work" at a game, and so should you. Games are delayed because the parent assigned to run the clock is at the door waiting to pay. That is just terrible.

Entrance fees can also be a hardship for grandparents. Perhaps someone should consider universal senior and military discounts at all youth basketball games.

You should not be shy or afraid to ask your son's coach for complimentary tickets (or passes) if you need them. You can also try to barter. Some coaches seem to need a helping hand with administrative and clerical work. It perplexes parents that we have to pay to attend our child's amateur sports games, while many make huge profits. However, we must admit that there are many teams and organizations that need financial help.

Parent Travel Expenses

This includes your gas, parking, tolls, flights, train, and bus fares, as well as hotel rooms and meals.

Food and Beverage

As with most venues, you cannot bring in outdoor food or beverages. Your financial support for the vending machines and concession stands is appreciated. My recommendation is to eat beforehand to save costs and avoid starving if you do not partake in the traditional youth basketball game cuisine: hotdogs, popcorn, potato chips, nachos, soft pretzels, along with candy, water, and sports drinks.

Carrying gum, mints, and nutrition bars also come in handy. Don't worry about your son eating before or after a game. Most coaches will have food for them in the locker room. I doubt our sons know this, but when players greet parents after a game with their food in hand, many parents' stomachs are probably growling.

Streaming Services
Look for free trials. Consider a monthly subscription for the basketball season and save money.

Team Gear

There is no greater support for a team than promoting them—especially at an away game. Parents, and any guests, should always be in team colors. Even if you receive free gear, you should budget for purchasing more. You should also ask your family and friends to do the same. Besides your son, I know the coaches will appreciate it.

Watching Games

Parents can scramble to watch youth basketball games on television and online. Most youth games are not live-streamed or available on demand. If you find one, you should plan to pay to watch. The NFHS Network ($79.99 annual pass or $11.99 monthly pass), which covers high school sports, is likely your best bet. You can find them at (nfhsnetwork.com). You can also find AAU games on fee-based streaming services. A few games are broadcast on radio stations. A team can also have multiple carriers, with multiple fees, during a single season.

Where You Can Find Youth Basketball Game Broadcasts:

- BallerTV (also broadcasts Nike EYBL games)
- BeTheBeast
- ESPN, including ESPN+ and ESPN2

- Flo Hoops
- FloTrack
- ITGNext

Two tips for finding live games to watch:

1. Search the team's social media page, website, and YouTube.
2. Surprisingly, I have watched a few games because students went live on social media. Once the game starts, you can search for the team's hashtag on YouTube, Facebook, and Instagram.

Medical Expenses

Be prepared to pay for health physicals required by most teams. If a coach does not ask for one, that is a red flag. You should also budget for a good dentist. It is reported that basketball players are prone to teeth injuries. Free and low-cost health insurance options are covered in Chapter VI.

Spending Money

Undoubtedly, your son will need money when he travels with his team. I had no idea these costs would add up substantially each year.

Stadium Seats

Long hours in a gym are part of a basketball parent's life. And since bleachers offer no support, I often remind myself to "sit up straight." At any rate, some intelligent people have created a great affordable invention called bleacher chairs! If you need relief, you can view the article, *The 14 Best Stadium Seats for Comfort and Support,* on hgtv.com to possibly find some comfort.

Rewards Parents Can Be Thankful For

Youth basketball brings joy to young people. They develop a well-rounded personality and learn team-building skills, which are tenets that will help them in their adult lives. Even through all the bad times, my family has priceless memories as we continue to watch the next generation play. Chad and I even created a special handshake when we greet each other at a game. It is something we will probably keep doing even after his basketball playing days end.

Watching Chad's tenacity is inspiring. He is self-driven, methodical, and patient. Every coach, trainer and member of academia continues to praise his wonderful disposition. I know that playing basketball has contributed significantly to that. It will likely do the same for your son.

Alleviation of Anti-Social Behavior

"Kids in sports, stay out of courts!"

This phrase dates back to at least 1952 when it appeared in an article titled *"News About Negroes"* by R.D. Armstrong.[12] It has been used in articles and court documents, while justifying that playing basketball effectively prevents young people from falling into anti-social behavior, violence, drug use, and crime-related behavior.

The Melting Pot

The youth basketball world is a melting pot of diversity. Basketball players meet people from all races, ethnicities, and socio-economic backgrounds. They also learn to have a worldview incredibly early in their lives.

Fashion

Basketball players have an extensive sneaker collection thanks to their teams. Today's sneakers are pricey, especially if your son needs an above-average size.

Parents will also save money on clothing. Outside of a special occasion, most young basketball players wear sweatsuits, hoodies, T-shirts, and shorts. They always seem ready to play basketball at any moment. Is it a coincidence that the NBA pre-game tunnel walk is a fashion show? Many players seem to like to dress to impress when they show up at work as adults. Perhaps, this occurs because they rarely dressed for anything besides playing basketball during their teenage and young adult years.

Travel Experiences

Players have many travel experiences. Generation Z basketball players are avid travelers. They have not only passed the travel experiences of their peers, but likely many of their parents at the same age. Asking Chad to name the cities and towns he has visited to play basketball is like playing a trivia game.

Try this with your own son if he has traveled extensively for basketball. Ask him to name the cities. In all likelihood, he may not remember. However, rephrase it and ask him the locations he has won or lost games. He may also remember the gym's name.

A travel benefit is that if your son plays on a sponsored team, all his expenses will be paid. You will likely never need to purchase any luggage. Players receive an abundance of nice travel duffel bags and luggage tags. The bags usually have the school, or team's name, along with a sponsor's logo, so they must stay in conformity and not bring personal luggage. They can carry their own knapsacks.

As a parent of a youth basketball player, do not be nervous about allowing your son to travel with "his" coach and "his" team. Coaches and chaperones are formidable in this area and willing to share the itinerary "if you ask." If your son is flying, you can use a live flight tracker (flightaware.com) or @sportsaviation (Twitter), which allows you to see real-time flight routes. The mode and style of travel will depend on the team's budget.

Teams travel via charter buses, private vans, airplanes, and carpooling. Oddly, I cannot recall when Chad traveled on Amtrak for basketball. You should set aside emergency money if you must travel to pick up your son from an away game, or to get him home.

Anything can happen, including an injury, another medical reason, or schedule changes.

When Chad was 14 years old, to save money, or the flight was overbooked, he was not able to travel home with his grassroots team from a tournament in Las Vegas. Instead, his coach sent him to ride with another coach and his players. They were going to drive to Los Angeles—through the desert—at night, and Chad would take a flight from there. Chad called to tell me of the new travel plans as he was getting ready to step into the car. I told Chad I would book him a flight home, and he should thank the coach for the offer. We were lucky that my cousin Al was also at the tournament and could take him to the Las Vegas airport.

Chad and I had a serious conversation when he got home about him jumping into anyone's ride. From then on, I budgeted to ensure that I, or my daughter, could travel to any away tournaments. Although travel benefits young basketball players, I only had to experience being absent once to understand that you, or an adult family member, may need to be with your son as much as possible. You may also need to confirm all travel plans "To and from..."

School Expenses

It has also been a significant blessing that I have not had to purchase textbooks, or other school supplies, for Chad since he started playing basketball.

Young Black Men and the Police

The sad reality for Black parents of sons in America is the constant worry of whether the police will harm them. Basketball parents have tall sons who are quickly noticed in public. If you have ever had the chance to see the movie, *Cornbread, Earl and Me*, you can probably relate.

I have learned that police officers and many others, regardless of race, ethnicity, or gender, are huge fans of young basketball players. Chad has shared that police officers are among the kindest people he encounters in public. Once he relayed that, I began to take notice. Police officers positively acknowledge him. They say hello, wave, nod, smile, and ask about his team. They wish him luck and all the best. A Washington D.C. Metro police officer once allowed me to record a conversation he and Chad had at the Black Lives Matter Plaza in Washington, D.C. A simple hello continued into a long talk covering everything from good sportsmanship to dialogue on ending youth gun violence. And of course, they discussed basketball and whether the

Washington Wizards would make the NBA Finals that year. It was good to learn that youth basketball has the support of law enforcement. I was reminded of the Police Athletic League (PAL) in New York City and the National Association of Police Athletic/Activities whose officers "work nationwide promoting the prevention of juvenile crime and violence by building relationships among kids."

Medical Care

Some physicians try to give the best care and follow-up, whether in an emergency room or a specialized center. I also think they have taught me more about human anatomy than I ever learned in any science class.

Community Service and Cultural Experiences

As a part of teaching life skills, many sports teams conduct community service activities. Basketball teams are no different. Prep schools have volunteer days. Good AAU teams may take players on cultural excursions. Even if a team does not provide this, you can find community service activities for your son, especially during the year-end holidays and the summer (in early-mid August when teams rarely play).

Chad has participated in spending the day playing basketball with formerly homeless veterans sponsored by Morgan Stanley, feeding families in a soup kitchen, shoveling snow for seniors, and helping a nonprofit with IT support. Community service is also a plus for college applications.

Dream Chaser

Several studies report that "Children appreciate the participation and interest of parents in monitoring their sport educational activities, but that parents must be alert and aware of their engagement so that the experience of their children in the sport context can be positive."[13]

An article in *Sports Psychologist* entitled, *The Coach / Parent / Athlete Relationships*[14] suggests there are three types of sports parents:

1. ***Under involved families***, the parents show little to no interest in the child's sport, talent, or progress.
2. ***Moderately involved*** athlete families balance firm parental direction with the child's power to make her or his own decisions about goals, participation, and commitment.
3. ***Overinvolved parents*** are emotionally involved with the child's sport experiences and performance, and tend to project their lives into their child's sport successes.

Parents should ask themselves, "Am I pushing my child through basketball?" "Is basketball my dream or theirs?" Parents should not live vicariously through their children. They cannot want success more than the player. For your child to grow into adulthood successfully with independent thoughts and character, you as a parent should let them decide their journey.

Then there are critics who may confuse your encouragement or having a strategy with using force on your son.

I am a huge basketball follower. I have been a fan of the Los Angeles Lakers since the 1980s when James Worthy #42 was my favorite player. The Atlanta Hawks and the New York Knicks are tied for 2nd. I have won a community service award from the Atlanta Hawks, which was presented to me during half-time with an arena full of people.

I also have a ton of NBA and college players I watch and cheer on, including my niece and nephew. It comes naturally that I am my son's biggest fan. I love watching him play, even more so because I can remember all the times when I had to help keep his chin up. There was actually a time when he did not believe he would ever dunk a ball or block a shot. I can recall the time, date and location he succeeded for the first time. Among the greatest joys of parenting is when your child says, "I did it."

People often confuse my participation, as if I was forcing Chad to play, or worse, he was only playing to appease me. If they knew what Chad has been through. How he has overcome adversity—as well as working hard despite his critics, one would understand how proud and honored

I am to share his accolades. Young people need to know that their parents love and support them without reservation.

There is no way a parent, or anyone else, can push a kid through basketball once they reach a certain age. Maybe that worked when Generation Z and Baby Boomers were kids, but it will certainly not work on this new generation.

Research states most kids quit sports at 13 years old. In youth basketball, I believe it is about 16 years old. Most parents know that even for kids who are not playing basketball, the teen years can be rebellious and challenging. If a parent must yell or constantly complain to their child about something sports-related, they may want to rethink whether it is something he, or she, wants to do. The reality is that only some players will get a trophy, and some teams will lose.

What happens to a kid who is being pushed into playing basketball, but does not want to be there? He will let you know because he will likely quit on his own. Or if he does not stop, parents may find themselves forcing them to practice, games, or workouts. If you have to force your son to play basketball—let it go, it is not worth the stress, frustration, or the money. The passion for playing basketball is internal, not external.

Your son's heart must be in the game. I cannot think of anything I could have done to make Chad awake at 5 am to run before school or be the last one in the gym at night. I cannot think of any punishment that would make him lift weights 3-4 times a week. No yelling in the world could force my nearly 7-foot-tall son to turn down a steak to eat a salad.

A young man plays basketball because he wants to, or he will rebel, where it matters the most—on the court. Chad knows it would not be debated if he ever decided he was done with basketball. I also have no intention of being a future employee for "The Venning Machine," as he is dubbed, should he become a professional player. I will always be mommy first, which has always been my favorite title.

Yes, some parents may be guilty of attempting to live vicariously through their children. Some may have hidden agendas. However, I think they are in the minority—or at least that is how it is projected. Most of us are only helping our sons chase their dreams, which all parents should do, whether their child is playing sports or otherwise.

Parents as a Positive Influence

Parents set the standards for their children. They should be the most influential people in a child's life. This fact is especially true in the world of youth basketball. Unfortunately, parents are accused of ruining youth sports. There are parent fights at games, and even murder has occurred for something as minuscule as a lack of playing time.[15]

Parents must do better. Youth sports are not worth getting arrested, or worse. Far too many adults in youth basketball are pushing the wrong narrative. Coaches will have a parent believe their son can get to the NBA, even though their son has not yet played a college game.

Parents seem to have a sense of entitlement. If their son is an elite player, they feel he is owed something. Although nearly half of active NBA players have at least one other elite athlete in their family,[16] no one is guaranteed anything in basketball. Even if you get your son through the door, he will have to work to stay there and progress.

Parents must keep their kids grounded and set realistic expectations. Parents should be encouraging and supportive, but not overbearing.

A Coaches Diary, which has over 10,000 followers on Instagram asked basketball Hall of Famer Dawn Staley, "What is the biggest difference between what the modern athlete has to deal with versus when you were an athlete?" Staley, who has been in basketball for 22 years, and is currently the head coach of the South Carolina Gamecocks, stated it was the parents.

"Parents are super invested, which is great, they love their kids, they want a return on their investment because they put a lot of money into their children to play in AAU, to have trainers so they're invested you know. If you put your money in the stock market, they are like watching it every day and that can be a detriment. You see it go up and down, and up and down, and then you're on the roller

coaster,[an] emotional roller coaster. You know sometimes you just have to sit back and let it grow. What I find [that] is pretty hard for me to swallow is that they don't want their children to hurt or to be uncomfortable."

Sometimes, your son may want to quit. What is your plan if he does? It is okay to let him know that there are many other career options besides playing basketball, including other lucrative sports careers with excellent salaries.

Erik "Coach Spo" Spoelstra, the head coach of the Miami Heat, started as the team's video coordinator and is now considered one of the top 15 coaches in the history of the NBA. Not bad for a former point guard who played at the University of Portland where he graduated with a communications degree, and then went to box shoes in a Nike warehouse.[17]

Tips on Being a Positive Sports Parent

- **Give Love:** It truly does conquer all.

- **Support their efforts**: It is human nature to embrace a smile from another and an encouraging word. Children need it the most. Parent's voices are internalized in their children. They will never forget your words and the way they made them feel. And they will remember those words throughout their entire lives. Do not mock your children if they struggle in basketball, because they will learn to never share their struggles with you. There will be others who will focus on any weaknesses your son may bring to the court. Support your son by focusing on his strengths.

- **Have Fun:** There is the fun before "the business" of basketball. Basketball is still a game of entertainment to be enjoyed.

- **Let Your Son Establish His Own Goals**: If he wants to work on having a better three-point shot, do not pressure him to work on his dribbling. Let his experience come organically.

Make suggestions, but never pressure, or punish him, if he disagrees with you. Research also states that basketball fathers "may have a negative emotional impact on the child as he often dominates the role of the second coach, which may lead to unnecessary pressure on the child."18

- **Reinforce positive behavior and teamwork.**
- **Encourage good sportsmanship and loyalty to his teammates.**
- **Never bash your son in front of his teammates.** That is likely one of the largest dream killers for any young basketball player. Many quit because they are too embarrassed to face their peers.
- **Success:** Your child's success on the court or lack thereof does not define you as a parent. If he fails at basketball, it does not mean he is a failure. Nor does it mean you are not successful as a parent.
- **Motivation:** Always remember you are your child's biggest motivator.
- **Win or Lose**, they should never feel defeated.

The Sidelines

Lights! Camera! Action! It is the time for players to take the stage.

This is what basketball is about. It is the fun and excitement in one of America's favorite pastimes. You hear the buzzer, players are at tip-off, and you're feeling the vibe. You hope your son plays well, and you want his team to win. Then boom! As if some magical button was pressed, parents start yelling at their kids, the coaches, and the referees.

Parents and other family members might be asked to leave. Not to mention the physical altercations which can seem to happen at any time. This is the absolute worst part of the sidelines.

Why is it difficult for some parents to sit and enjoy the game without being obnoxious? Excitement is one thing, but being annoying is another. Todd Wolfson, the head basketball coach at St. Francis High School has put parents on notice and tweeted, "It's a HUGE gym. Please don't sit a row or two behind your son/daughters bench. Go sit somewhere else."

And no, parents should not be yelling "get yours" at their son. That mentality is selfish, and it sets a bad example in basketball. That mindset usually does not work out well for that player, or his team. From a parent's perspective, here is what I believe is the number one rule regarding your son's on-the-court play: Do not get involved! You should allow the coaches and referees to do their jobs. Many coaches have huge egos. Many will not want to admit they may be wrong. Referees are human and make mistakes. Parents must stop blaming the referees or coaches for their son's performance on the court. These are factors beyond a spectator's control. The worst thing a parent can do is embarrass their son, a coach, a referee, or anyone else during a game.

If you speak ill of the coach at a game, even to the person sitting next to you, you should assume it will always get back to him (or her). As a parent of a basketball player, you should be aware that from the time your kid hits the court, even if you are in the smallest town in the smallest state in the USA, someone is watching and listening to your son *and* you.

Your courtside manner is important. Disruptive parents are rarely forgotten. Then parents are surprised and may ask, "Why isn't my son getting exposure?" "Why isn't my son getting any offers?" "Why is my son's playing time short?" You have now forgotten what impact you may have had.

As parents, if you strike out your kid, coaches may sympathize with them, but attitude problems from parents do not go unnoticed. There can be silent consequences, retaliation, and exclusion. The youth basketball world is small—there may be one degree of separation from your son's coach to a college coach. Coaches attend national conferences together and talk, even if they are rivals. There are websites for coaches only.

When I asked, none of them would confirm or deny whether they kept notes in them on unruly parents. In a conversation with a D1 college coach, I asked whether he knew a particular parent who was my friend. He answered with a look of frustration.

"Yes, I remember her. She was always the one screaming at me from the stands." Is it a coincidence that her son did not last at that college, and he was forced to leave at the end of the season under the auspices that he was ready for a higher level?

Coaches are eerily quiet when it comes to giving parents feedback. They will not pull you to the side regarding negative behaviors. In college, many head coaches do not speak one-on-one with their players or parents. They leave that job to the assistant coaches.

One relayed to me, "We are making them into men, we do not have time to call mommy."

Receiving any communications from a head coach is equivalent to getting a call from a school's principal, or a school president. It is rarely with good news.

We cannot blame coaches or referees the way they treat parents. How would you feel if someone showed up to your job screaming interrupting your workday?

Entitlement has no place in youth sports. What I have learned, is that the less negative attention you bring to yourself, the better. Your son is in the game, not you.

Embarrassing Your Child Should Never Be A Service You Offer

These are recommendations for parents to consider as they walk through youth basketball circles.

1. The coaching world is full of tall, dark, and handsome men and beautiful women. Mothers should never date their son's coach. Fathers should not flirt with a coach's wife or girlfriend. Do not become the topic of gossip or place your son in a position to receive hurtful remarks from other players.
2. If a coach flirts with you, use caution. They may be assessing your integrity or are trying to recruit your son from another team. Keep your interactions professional.
3. Women should dress practical to reduce distractions.
They also should be aware they may be in the company of young men at the age of raging hormones. You do not want anyone to question, "Whose mother is that?"
4. Don't be the hook-up. Refrain from bringing your daughter, or another young woman, to try and snag a player.
5. On the road, refrain from visiting your son's hotel room, which he will likely be sharing with a teammate. Let him know your

room number, or meet him in the lobby. No one wants their mom (or dad) knocking on their room door.

6. Never visit the locker room or another area where the team assembles without permission, as this seems to embarrass players.
7. Do not join the conversation while coaches speak with your son, or his team.
8. Game attendees will talk about the players. You may be sitting next to someone with a negative opinion of your son. Ignore them. Do not take it personally, and do not respond.
9. Refrain from posting controversial comments on social media, which include negative remarks about a team's owner, coach, or referee.
10. Players have also shared that they prefer if parents "like" a post (about them or their team) but do not post comments under them. You can share a post about your son on your page. Be careful how you engage with "fans" on social media who will like your son when he is playing well, but may change up when he is not.
11. Keep your family controversies off of social media. It is embarrassing and you may be mentally hurting your child.
12. Pre-Game: Players are getting in their zone before a game.
    Do not contact your son when it is close to game time. Coaches have strict rules preventing players from using their phones before a game. If you communicate before a game, keep it simple. No player needs their parent in their head during a game. Words such as "Good luck," "I'm proud of you." "I love you." "Do your best and remember to have fun." "Listen to your coach," should suffice.
13. Post-Game: The game is over. The gym is clearing out. There are areas where parents, family members, and friends are allowed to wait for players. Try not to walk on or across the court, and do not go to the locker room. Be cordial with any security personnel.
    Be patient! You can easily wait up to an hour! While parents and others are waiting, your son is in a "team meeting," celebrating a victory, or possibly being chastised for a loss. Use this as an opportunity to speak with other parents and greet people waiting to support your son.

14. After the game, ask your son these simple "let's keep it light" questions if you want to keep up. "Did you give your best effort?" "Did you have fun?" "Are you caught up with your school assignments?"
15. Players usually travel to and from games with their team. If your son wants to travel with you, he must get permission from his coach. Advise your son to never leave a game or practice alone. Also, if your son leaves with you and no one notices, that may be a problem you may want to investigate.

- Purchase your son's domain name. For example, chadvenning.com.
- You can also create a website, or a YouTube channel, for highlights so you can have a link readily available to send to college recruiters.

Documenting The Journey

Since I became a mother, I have documented every milestone in my kids' lives through photos, videos, and those adorable baby books. My kids have nicknamed me, "Momarazzi" because I have taken post-game photos of Chad with any family members (or friends) who attended any of his high school and AAU games.

When Chad was in the 9th grade, I also purchased a domain in his name, created his website, and an email account. His website included his stats, photos, highlight videos, educational information, and his coach's contact information. When any college coach requested information, we saved time by sending a private link.

Making your own videos is also helpful for your son. I have made videos from pre-game warm-ups, which come in handy if you do not have any film for your son. In warm-ups, you can capture some good moves from players. Getting to the warm-up, which usually takes place 15-30 minutes before a game, will also ensure that you will not be late for the tip-off. It is also an excellent time to introduce yourself to courtside photographers and videographers. You can follow up with them to see if they will share any footage of your son, or you can check their online accounts.

Chad also used my videos for review during the ride home. By the time the game was over, I had already texted him his footage. It was something I did all the way up to the end of his first college season. Now, he is in the habit of reviewing his game immediately post-game.

If you can, remember to record the game at home. You may learn a great deal from the commentators and game highlights, which is something you miss while attending games in person. You can also learn the game's media sponsors, and your family can possibly support them.

Organizing It All

Organizational tips to save time and keep you prepared.

- **Game Schedule**: Print and post them on your refrigerator, or some place you see it daily. You may have to find the schedule yourself on a team's website or social media. Coaches do not have a habit of sharing schedules with parents. Most of the time, your son may not know his own schedule because he will find out in team meetings and at practice.
- **Vehicle Box:** Snacks, water, aspirins, first-aid kit, air freshener, socks, face cloths, towels, toothbrush, toothpaste, blanket, travel pillow, lotion, T-shirt, umbrella, and extra sneakers and shorts for your son. A change of clothes for yourself, portable charger, books (reading materials), sunglasses, plastic cutlery, straws, writing pads/pens, and in a COVID world, face masks and hand sanitizer.

Parent Protection

Once upon a time, in urban communities, players were revered and protected. At least that was how it was for me growing up in New York City during the 1970s and 1980s. Everyone was proud of the young basketball players. There was a code in the streets for them and any other young person, who had a shot of "making it." Even the most feared criminals would protect them.

Unfortunately, we now live in a different world. A world where public acclaim and even the slightest possibility of wealth can put a target on their back. Everyone will not be comfortable with your son's success, perceived or otherwise.

> *"You cannot kick it with the same dudes you kicked it with. You cannot associate in the same realms that you associated with. [You're going to] have to change if you expect change."*[19]
> *Deion Sanders*

Let your son know to stay away from potential harmful people at all costs—especially the ones with nothing to lose. Players should also be careful and remain alert when playing in, and leaving, from outdoor tournaments. They should stay aware of their surroundings when casually hanging out in high-crime neighborhoods, even though they may feel a kinship. I was also distrustful of anyone who creates funny, but not really funny, nicknames for a player. The tongue can be very revealing.

Parents also need to caution their sons that some of their peers may be envious, and even grown men might be jealous of them. When you find that parents are attacking players in games held in church gyms, nothing is sacred. Even coaches are fighting one another, and lousy sportsmanship is everywhere. This is highly troubling and disrespectful to the legacy and the vision had by the creator of the game, James Naismith. His rules for basketball stated the need for everyone to have respect.

> *"Let us all be able to lose gracefully and to win courteously; to accept criticism as well as praise; and last of all, to appreciate the attitude of the other fellow at all times."*[20]

Balancing Life

Whatever you may remember about your high school experience likely consists of hanging out with your friends afterschool, going shopping, attending parties, going to the movies, falling in puppy love, and having long summers without a care. The lives of teen basketball

players are vastly different. They have a limited social life in which they forgo many things that are automatic for other young people.

Chad was already 17 years old when he attended his first teen party. It was a celebration from his friends before he left for prep school. The party was so important to him that he declined an invitation to attend the NBA draft that year. I have also realized he has not had a birthday celebration with family in years because it occurs at the start of the fall basketball season.

Other parents would inquire, "How do you keep Chad in the house on a weekend night?" "How do you determine his curfew?" Trust me, it was not hard. When my son had to get up at dawn, seven days a week, to run or study before practice, he set his own schedule. Chad taught me that any player who has the time to party, or stay out late, is not fully invested in basketball. Friends, or family members their age, probably only engage with them on social media, or when they are playing video games remotely. Their teammates, who become like brothers and possible life-long friends, are the members of their social circle.

Young basketball players rarely travel anywhere alone, and if they do, it is not often. They always have a buddy system. Yet, adults must not forget that they are still young. They want to learn to drive, go shopping, go to the movies, attend school socials, and have fun like other teens, or so I thought.

Although Chad attended his junior prom, he did not attend his high school prom because he was physically exhausted. For this book, I asked Chad to tell me what basketball players do in their spare time. He replied, "The same as regular kids—workouts and anything they like to do. I play video games to relax." Just the fact that he mentioned "regular" kids gives credence to my point.

Young basketball players are still regular kids, although their lives are structured differently. And although America struggles with exercising, especially among children who sit in front of screens more than playing on grass, Chad seems to think that workouts are a routine part of life. I am sure all young athletes are conditioned like this, and perhaps they cannot miss something they have never had.

As parents, we must help our kids keep a healthy balance. It should not always be "work, work, work." Because before you know it, they will be at the end of their childhood.

The Circle of Trust: Family, Friends, and Others

Family and the support of friends is an excellent thing to have. Who would not want their kids to be supported by siblings, uncles, aunts, grandparents, and cousins? Parents should welcome their prayers and good wishes. Although they may have good intentions, you should never allow them to speak on behalf of you, or your son, in basketball circles. Family and friends, without realizing it, can also be harsh critics. Many of them do not realize the last thing we want to hear is criticism when our son may not have performed well in a game, or his team lost.

My phone stayed busy when Chad fumbled or had a bad game. My advice is to ignore anyone who makes it a habit of sending negative energy to you. It is said that "In prosperity, our friends know us, in adversity, we know our friends."

Family and friends may also ask you for freebies. I have been asked for free tickets, sneakers, and team gear. Once, I was even asked to provide a complimentary hotel room. I am not sure what message is going out in the universe about youth basketball to others. None of that $19 billion in the youth athletic industry is going to the parents—and if it does, it is illegal.

Then there was a time when Chad was not responding to a family member. After one of his games, they sent me a message stating, "Tell Chad to call me back!" I am assuming she wanted to share her thoughts on his performance. I thought Chad is 19 years old, and I am not his agent. I also cannot make him call anyone—especially after a game.

The most-asked question is from someone who has never attended a game but always wants to know when the next one is so they can attend. How many basketball parents can relate?

Becoming Guarded

I have noticed that the nuclear basketball family becomes closed and guarded if they believe there may be a future NBA player on deck. It is likely motivated by money. The irony is that a young player destined for wealth may not yet have the financial literacy to understand it all himself. Sometimes it feels like a young basketball player is on his own when he reaches a certain level from playing basketball.

The distrust of others begins early in the lives of talented young basketball players. I do not know of any other career path in which teenagers, or young adults, are faced with trying to discern who is trustworthy so profoundly. They have the mental and psychological agility that no other sport requires—although football may be a close second.

Coaches, who are adults, may also never realize the effect they may have on a young person when they lie, stretch the truth, or withhold it from them while serving in their mentoring role.

The Handlers

Parents should watch out for the handlers who serve as quasi, unlicensed sports agents to young players. Chad had one by 10th grade. He just appeared and I truly thought he was going to help us. When we disagreed on a small matter, he lost his temper. He proceeded to argue with me in the middle of a gym after one of Chad's games. I let him vent and then kindly reminded him that Chad was my son and not a stepping stone for him.

Every handler I have ever met (or heard about, with other young players and "their mothers") were all making career moves for themselves while allegedly "promoting" a basketball prospect. They live off of the vulnerabilities of parents and the eagerness of players.

Telling a coach that they can bring a player to a team if offered a job is not beneath them. Meanwhile, they are sharing with parents how much that coach wants their son.

When handlers work for the good, you can have an extra person promoting your son to their network. Those who are unethical join the ranks of those affecting the well-being of young people and may bring conflict to a family. When the pieces are broken and, on the floor, who is picking them up and repairing any damage? The parents.

Your conversations with your son on trust and how to interact with others will be essential.

Siblings

The time you spend with your son while he is playing basketball can bring siblings together, or place a wedge between them. Parents of multiple children should ensure basketball does not monopolize their attention from their other children. Sibling rivalry and sibling jealousy can be a detriment within a family. Try to keep everyone connected and include the entire household in your process unless someone opts out.

Team Parents

In the early years (elementary and middle school) basketball parents share information, schedule carpools, help fundraise, and may even take turns with after-game snack purchases. Chad was once in a book club organized by another basketball parent. While the kids were reading a new book, parents would bond over wine and appetizers. Pre-game, fathers would tailgate in the parking lots. Parents shared pick-ups and drop-offs. We became a surrogate family.

As time passes and kids go further in youth basketball, team parents remain cordial, but for reasons which still perplex me, some grow distant. They turn into competitors and may be envious if your son is excelling over theirs. Others seemed to have joined a secret society. Quite a few begin to exhibit an air of conceit based on their son's status and attention. They will look down on parents whose sons may not have an "elite" status. Those attitudes trickle down to the players and add to the reasons why coaches struggle to get together a team spirit. These parents do not care if the team wins or loses as long as their child plays and scores. They will brag and possibly tease another child on the team. In turn, their child may display an egotistic demeanor and connect their success on the court to their self-importance.

Phil Jackson, one of the greatest coaches in NBA history, wrote in his book *Eleven Rings: The Soul of Success* that,

> **"Winning was fine—in fact, my mother was one of the most fiercely competitive people I've ever met—but reveling in your own success was considered an insult to God."**

Parents can also take on phony tendencies. Although not the majority, I have had parents who would only speak to me when Chad had a great game or was featured in the media. A basketball parent could go an entire season without any other parent even saying one word to

COACHES & PARENTS WORKING TOGETHER

them if their son is not a standout on the court. They will, however, stare if they see the coach or another influencer speaking with you.

Even if a team hosts a parent gathering event, parents stay in a clique or off to themselves. They will pretend they do not know the answers to questions other parents may ask.

One story I vividly remember, and likely will never forget, is when Chad was in the 10th grade. Neither of us knew the steps to take to obtain a basketball scholarship for him. Outside of quizzing family members and scouring the internet for hours, I can admit we were in the dark.

One day, I had the opportunity to speak with another basketball mother whose son had several D1 college offers. We were having an engaging conversation. She rambled about how would to be difficult for her son to select one college. She was also trying to decide whether he should go into the G League. Those are options youth basketball players and parents dream of.

I asked, "How were you able to obtain so many offers?"

She grew quiet.

As I noticed the awkward silence, I asked, "You probably have so much information that could help others on this road like me?"

"To be honest, I do not care about others. My kid has his scholarship coming. All I know is I won't have to pay for college, "she blurted.

She *actually* said that. From that point on, whenever we spoke, her words seemed carefully crafted, as if she would accidentally slip me useful information.

In another interaction with her, we were speaking after a game. Chad, who was projected as the underdog, really played well.

I said, "Chad did his thing today against x player."

She responded by sharing information about Chad's competition. "Well, you know x player started late in basketball, so…" She caught herself and stopped talking, probably because of the surprised look on my face.

THE PARENT'S SECTION: OUTSIDE THE LOCKER ROOM

Without reservation, some basketball parents can be brutal not only in your face but behind your back as well. You must learn to ignore a great deal of negative energy and comments.

Leader Johnson, a senior writer & draft analyst for the NBA Draft Room, has tweeted about those parental types:

> ***"When parents of kids that are ranked hit me up about other kids, they say they do not deserve the credit you gave them. That type of hating is not tolerated in my inbox. I won't listen to it and will check you at the door."***

I knew exactly what he meant. "People want you to do good, but never better than them."

Basketball is a team sport— There is no 'I" in team. If all parents care about is what their child can do, or what they have, basketball coaches suggest they take them to an individualized sport like tennis or golf. Parents should always help one another and not try to hinder opportunities for other young people. If you are a parent, help another one out.

Not all parents can make it to games, so maybe you can go live for them and show their son playing. Not all have vehicles. Maybe you can offer a ride. Not all understand the dynamics of youth basketball. If something worked for you, why not share it with others?

For years, when Chad was in high school, if his teammates needed a pickup, or a ride home, I would provide one. There were late-night drop offs, which included school nights. Those rides also included stopping at a store for them. If anyone did not have money, I would treat them. During all those rides, even though I had their child in my car, not one parent ever called to speak with me, let alone say thank you. However, I would make sure their child called them. You would be hard-pressed to find a youth basketball parent who does not need a favor or information. I am grateful to anyone who has ever helped me and Chad.

A few times one summer, Ryan Peek, the father of Hayden Peek (NYU), would drive an hour from their home to meet us on Staten Island. He would then go another 90 minutes to take our kids to practice. He would not accept a cent from me, and trust me, I tried. Those few weeks made an enormous difference in the world to me and Chad.

I want to believe most basketball parents mean well. Most are learning just like you and me. Contrary to popular belief, not all basketball parents or their young players have a desire to go pro. Nor are they competing for social media acclaim. Basketball could simply be a recreational activity and a positive experience for their child. No parent should worry about another parent wishing ill will on their son. All parents should be kind to one another because there is a saying that, "Blowing out someone else's candle will never make yours shine brighter." Whatever good God has for your son, he will likely obtain it.

Basketball parents will meet squanders, phonies, and scammers—they should not be one of them. The irony is that NBA parents are some of the nicest and humblest people I have ever met. Their unselfishness and willingness to help other parents (including those with young players), is to be commended.

When Prayers Go Up, Blessings Come Down

When I learned that James Naismith gave up the ministry to "preach clean living through sport," it made perfect sense to me that the success of basketball worldwide is no coincidence.

If you are a believer, you already know that prayer changes things. I love listening to NBA player Chris Paul (Phoenix Suns) discuss how his family constantly prays for him. At the start of every game, Giannis Antetokounmpo (Milwaukee Bucks) says a prayer. Stephen Curry (Golden State Warriors) and former NBA player Kyle Korver discuss their faith publicly. They are great role models not only for basketball sons but for all sons (and daughters). Youth basketball teams may also pray together. Of course, depending on your family's religious beliefs, your child may opt-out.

The first time Chad received a business card from someone who could possibly help him in the future, I was advised to "Take that home and put it in your Bible."

"Faith is the confidence that what we hope for will actually happen.; it gives us assurance about things we cannot see."
Hebrews 11:1.

Never wane.

All basketball parents can be MVPs and should remember to have a team spirit off the court, as much as their child should on the court. Do not let them, their coach, or their teammates down.

Let's work to change the negative perceptions and all try to be on #TeamParents.

CHAPTER II

COACHES & PARENTS WORKING TOGETHER

"A Coach must never forget that he is a leader and not merely a person with authority."

— John Wooden (1910 – 2010)

The definition of a coach is an athletic instructor or trainer. A youth basketball coach is also a mentor, scheduler, travel coordinator, psychologist, fundraiser, supervisor, babysitter, referee, marketing pro, game guardian, and a winning team developer. They possess a high basketball IQ and love the game of basketball. They rarely seem to strive for personal fame or notoriety. They make tremendous sacrifices, including:

- Spending their own money to help young people.
- Serving as a mentor to many young men who may not have other positive role models.
- Moving their families for employment opportunities.

COACHES & PARENTS WORKING TOGETHER

- The need to follow various everchanging rules from high school leagues, basketball governing bodies, the AAU, school administrators, and funders.

- Coaches also have a high divorce rate. They spend so much time away from their families that some refer to wives as "coaching widows."

It surprised me that most youth basketball coaches may not earn a livable wage. For that alone, they deserve high praise and appreciation. A wonderful way to thank them for their service is to give the head coach and his staff a year-end holiday, or birthday gift. This will also teach your son the meaning of gratitude.

Although coaches all have a similar goal, which is to win games, parents should know there are differences among them.

High School Coaches

Salary.com reports the average high school basketball coach's salary is $55,583. Compare that to Hank Carter, the highest-paid high school football coach, whose salary is $158,512.[21] I know high school coaches in private and parochial schools who are paid $5,000 (or less) a season.

High school coaches and their staff are usually educators who have teaching, or school administrator, degrees. Besides coaching, they may hold another position in the school. Their staff may include assistant coaches, student managers, and a team mascot (who parents should also consider thanking). With all their responsibilities, you should be aware that many high school coaches lack the time to map out a personal basketball future for every player. High school coaches do not receive any financial award or incentive for getting their players a scholarship. Nor are they sanctioned if they do not.

Coach Staff Gift Ideas:

The Mamba Mentality: How I Play by Kobe Bryant
A food basket, restaurant and other gift cards. Any items with the words "A Great Coach," "#1 Coach," such as on key chains, a mug, or T-shirt. Travel items such as luggage tags.

Paul Biancardi, ESPN's national recruiting director, says,

> *"Coaches need to know that they need to help with the process. You must take part in your player's recruitment. You have to advise them through the process. If they are not getting recruited, you have to help them get recruited and if they're not going to get recruited, but have a desire just to play, then get them a walk-on situation. I was a walk-on so I understand that anybody can become a walk-on if you want it, and you want it badly. There is a home for everyone in the game."*[22]

High school coaches are the ones who take care of the "student" in the term student-athlete. They will likely succeed in getting your son to graduation and into college (regardless of their basketball skills). They have college admission knowledge but may lack formidable connections to college basketball coaches.

Off the court, a high school coaching staff's most important tasks are to ensure your son is on track with governing body timelines, registrations, and deadlines, such as those from the National Collegiate Athletic Association (NCAA). This topic is covered in Chapter V.

It is essential that you, as a parent, meet with them and have a plan if your son plays on a high school team. Your son should also ensure he communicates with his high school coach if he connects with college coaches. A high school coach's opinion carries a lot of weight with college coaches. The high school coach will likely be the first person a college coach reaches out to, even before your son, his AAU coach, and definitely before a parent.

Because a coach has the option of not informing you if any college coaches have reached out on behalf of your son, you should request the high school coach contact you immediately if it occurs.

Grassroots and AAU Coaches

These coaches are likely independent contractors who work in basketball part-time during the spring and summer basketball seasons. They may earn $25-$50 per hour, or a yearly base salary of

$25,000-$40,000. They are the ones who are interested in the "athlete" in the term

student-athlete. Their teams may be under a nonprofit corporation with a board of directors—which may include their family and friends. The head coach may be the executive director/president. A few NBA players have sponsored AAU teams.

As a nonprofit, if their tax filings are current, you can find their IRS 990 tax filings on ProPublica.org which will include their financial and leadership information.

Grassroots and AAU coaches are considered leaders in youth basketball due to their affiliations with sneaker brand companies and professional basketball players. They may also have outstanding athletic agility, are highly knowledgeable about the sport, and have an immense passion for basketball.

AAU and grassroots coaches are not reviewing high school transcripts to see if a player is on track to graduate (or their college eligibility). They recruit players fast and bench (or cut them) with equal speed. Their primary goal is to win games and championships in a short time period. If they are a sponsored team, when they lose games, it places their financial sponsorship at risk.

Depending on their team's resources, these coaches can open the door to professional-related basketball experiences for your son through travel, connecting with professional players, and playing in packed venues with a lot of press and publicity. However, there is no guarantee they will connect your son, or get him past that level for a college scholarship (or a professional career). They seem to stay in their lane during the spring and summer seasons.

Use the grassroots time to your advantage by networking with college coaches at games and tournaments during "live" periods when you have permission to contact them.

College Coaches

The head coach is the boss in every sense of the word and there is a clear hierarchy.

According to *USA Today*, the average salary for a D1 college head coach during the 2020-21 season was $2.7 million. That amount goes down substantially for D2 and JUCO colleges, but many still earn six figures. College coaches have no problem sharing how they will not jeopardize their job over a recruit, player, or their family. You and your son will need to understand that. There are tough and stringent regulations they must follow. There are severe consequences if they find themselves on the wrong side, including going to prison.

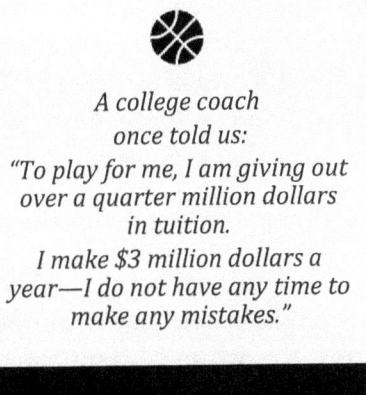

A college coach once told us:
"To play for me, I am giving out over a quarter million dollars in tuition.
I make $3 million dollars a year—I do not have any time to make any mistakes."

College basketball is also a big business. Parents must look at college coaches from the lens that you will be interacting with high-level business leaders who help oversee millions of dollars for their institution.

In the 2021-22 season, the University of Louisville (KY) received $48.5 million in athletic earned revenue. Their head coach, Kenny Payne's annual salary is $3.3 million.[23] That is comparable to an NBA head coach's salary, which averages between $2 million and $8 million per year.[24]

The recruiting process is likely the only time you will likely converse with a head coach. Even then, the NCAA has rules that limit contact. Let your son lead the conversation if you find yourself in a meeting with a college coach. They want to see if your son is in control of his own recruiting, which is covered more in Chapter V. Remember that they will be vetting you and your family as much as your son, even after they may have made an offer.

Coaches: In Control or Out of Control?

Many years ago, when I led a youth development organization, I hired an athletic director who also served as the basketball coach. Besides having a stellar coaching record, he was also a former player who excelled in high school and college. His references were impeccable. Seeing him as a role model for 11-12-year-old middle schoolers struck me as a wonderful idea.

One Friday afternoon, the team won the state championship.

The calls to my office began as I was preparing to leave for my weekend. Parents were on the phone screaming expletives and calling for the coach to be terminated. A few of them took the liberty to show up in my office with their crying kids still in their uniforms.

What could have gone wrong?

The parents said that after the game, the coach took the winning trophy and went home. He failed to congratulate the kids or celebrate with them. When I spoke to the coach, I informed him he had to return the trophy.

"This is my trophy, and I won the championship, not those kids," he said with authority.

My attempts at reasoning with him seemed to have fallen on deaf ears. I gave him an ultimatum—either bring the trophy back or be fired.

That Monday, he did return the trophy—but it was broken, and my assistant had to order a new one. We held a public ceremony to present our winning team to the community. At the event, that same coach took over the microphone and proclaimed his victory while grinning from ear to ear. The crowd booed him, and I felt nauseous.

Hopefully, you won't run into coaches with such egos, but they are out there. You must watch out for them and tread cautiously if one crosses your son's path.

The Power of Coaches

"The best coaches are those who inspire a player to be great. The one who a player can trust. If you believe in him, we know that young man will likely go far."
—Kenny "Coach Boobie" Jackson

Parents be warned. Coaches may not have the fortitude to make your son a star, or even a skillful player, but most have the power to prevent them from becoming one. Whether intentionally or unintentionally, in the blink of an eye, a coach can end your son's basketball journey and send him to the basketball cemetery.

They can use your son to propel other players. They can be so focused on one player that they do not invest in others. They can fill their rosters with players that they never had any intention of playing. If a coach's son, or another relative, is on the team—you should know they will get preferential treatment. Coaches can reduce playing time, knowing full well that obtaining game highlights at the high school level is needed for college recruitment. Their staff can miss important NCAA, or other governing bodies' deadlines. They can see your son struggling academically but will not share how bad grades will affect them down the road if they seek a college scholarship. They can give a bad reference to college coaches. And worst of all, they can kill your son's self-confidence which could transpose over into other areas of his life.

Then, one day, it is already the 12th grade, and your son may not have any scholarship offers or basketball plans. Your son is stressed and you, as a parent, may be wondering what went wrong.

Trust me, the confusion began way before the 12th grade. It is just that parents and players did not piece together the puzzle on being misled, or they just lacked the knowledge to counter it.

At the collegiate level, the NCAA and other governing bodies address grievances and complaints for allegations of using student-athletes and there are sanctions. Yet, few hold the leaders of the youth basketball world accountable.

If you have any intentions of basketball being a future endeavor for your son, the most important questions to ask are, "Where is this headed?" "What are your plans for my son?" Those are better questions than, "When will he start?" "Will he play?"

If parents ask those two questions, you will either get lied to or learn what you need to know. If the verbal answers do not suffice, or the coach seems to be dodging the question, their body language will likely speak for them. Most will likely laugh heartily and promise to get back to you. As a parent, you need to find out the priority of each of your son's coaches or trainers. Is it to develop your son to be a better player, a great student, and a great individual with good character? Is your son just a placeholder? Will they help him get to the next level if he is deserving of such? If you cannot get a definitive answer, or if your son is confused, it may be time to find other options for him.

Time is of the essence. It will be harder for your son to find another team than it is for a coach to find another player.

My curiosity always gets the best of me, and I wonder why we rarely hear professional players publicly thanking coaches from their youth basketball years. I have heard coaches complain about how much they had done for a player, yet they never came back and supported their organization. The lack of acknowledgment from players, who have moved up, is telling. Many coaches churn players in and out all of the time, and some are used as stepping stones for them.

As such, why are coaches surprised that players may share similar sentiments? After all, the adults indoctrinated in their minds early on that "It's just business."

Collaborating with Coaches

Many coaches resent parents. They believe parents cause too many problems. It is mind-boggling that some coaches fail to see the correlation that a player is our child who we are responsible for raising and ensuring they are always okay. Parents are the guardians of the game.

Young players have shared with me that once they are on a team, their coach's attitude is that parents do not have much usefulness. Yet, we are still working hard, even for coaches who spare no time in losing the proper business acumen regarding parents. They seem to have no problem in shaming parents in public. It has become a popular podcast subject and daily trend on social media. I would not be surprised if some of them are monetizing it.

You rarely hear or see a college, or a professional coach, with a similar agenda. Those coaches seem to have a tremendous amount of respect for the parents of athletes. How can parents collaborate with coaches who share commentary about parents stating, "You are not the star of the show. You are a member of the supporting cast. Move accordingly."

Besides the rudeness, the major issue I have is what "accordingly" means. Surely, coaches with these attitudes must know, with the exception of this book, there is no "guidebook" for basketball parents. I can almost bet you one million dollars the coach who posted that statement has failed to organize one parent meeting for his team.

In addition, coaches like him should be aware from a parental lens, no matter much the industry props up young basketball players, most parents do not see their children as stars in a show.

Coaches share negative sentiments but have no problem calling parents late at night, on weekends, or during the workday whenever they need something. They have no idea how intrusive and inconsiderate they can be. Parents are expected to answer promptly and hold long conversations. I have had to stop whatever I was doing many times to speak with, and provide documents to coaches. I can recall times when coaches had me so nervous that I was scared to reschedule meetings because I thought they would pass over Chad if I did. I almost forfeited a much-needed family trip because a coach wanted to make a last-minute home visit. The coach claimed to understand the reason, but I could tell it took away something from Chad's recruitment.

Coaches have also tried to pressure me to answer or speak for Chad when he was old enough to speak for himself. My steadfast rule is to remain "outside the locker room" as much as possible. I would share that I could not answer for Chad because, "I am not the one playing." That always seemed like an acceptable answer for them all.

My cousin Al told me coaches use this tactic because,

> *"A coach can reach out to the dad and the kid, but if the mom says no, it's a no. You must convince the mom before anything."*

Trust the Process | It's Just Business

"Trust the process" and "It's just business" are some of the most-used basketball phrases by coaches to parents and players. Trust the process means if a player works hard, they will succeed. It also means they should trust what is being told to them by coaches.

The actual term evolved from "The Process," a phrase coined by Sam Hinkie, the general manager of the Philadelphia 76ers from 2013 to 2016. The process was his plan to turn around the team with the League's worst record during his tenure. For the parents of youth basketball players, it has taken on an entirely different meaning.

Parent: "Do you think his jersey is the right size?"

Coach: "Trust the process, mom."

Parent: "Does your gym have a defibrillator?"

Coach: "Trust the process, dad."

Parent: "When will the game schedule be posted?"

Coach: "Trust the process."

Often, I wanted to ask a coach, "Exactly what is *your* process? "It amazes me that youth coaches have taken a phrase from an NBA team's general manager, turned it into something else, and thrust it upon young players and their parents.

"It's Just Business"

Throughout this book, you will also find several references to the phrase, "It's just business." Coaches use this term to relay disappointing news. They would like to believe they are setting young people up for the harsh realities of adulthood or helping their parents do so. Yet, for players and parents, there is no onboarding process. Players can be immediately terminated after being offered the job. Players do not know their benefits or how to qualify for a promotion. There is no human resources department to file a grievance. What they mean is,

> *"This is just how it is in youth basketball, and there is nothing you, or anyone else, can do about it. You can take your son someplace else because there are plenty waiting to fill his spot."*

Youth basketball parents are in a precarious situation. Coaches with integrity who provide honest answers to simple questions are the stars in the youth coaching realm. Parents should not give up! Ask your questions and seek your answers.

It is my hope that you will consider following the suggested Twitter accounts and podcasts in Chapter IX. There you will find several coaches who get communications with parents correct. They provide engaging dialogue and request positive feedback from parents.

Practice Time

Practice is a private and sacred time for your son and his team. If parents are allowed to attend, it is probably because they have provided transportation. Some parents watch practices intently. Some parents present body language, which shows how difficult it is for them to detach themselves from the court and coaching staff. They are fidgeting in their seat. They may be pacing up and down in front of other parents. They are mumbling under their breath and trying to make eye contact with their son. Or they are talking excessively about what the coaching staff is doing wrong.

Coaches, on the other hand, run their practices as if no spectators are there. I love their intent focus on their players. Yet, they can be animated. They may curse, scream, and stomp their feet. They will challenge their players in ways you may disagree with. What they will not do is engage with you during practice or after.

Have you ever noticed that coaches are in a hurry to leave after practice or a game? They are usually the first ones off the court. The exception may be when they have to give a media interview, and even

COACHES & PARENTS WORKING TOGETHER

then, they are brief. At the end of practice, let the coach leave so they can continue their day (or night) and get home to their family.

You may not agree with everything you see or hear, but you should remain silent because what you say or do can be used against your son. The head coach may not notice what parents are doing, but you better believe someone else is there watching your every move—and that someone else could be the coach's wife.

For me, practice hours meant two things: sleep or boredom. I like to see the cake at the end, I do not want to watch it baking. I also in no way, shape, or form ever wanted to distract Chad at practice.

When I was not watching Chad develop, I used the time to run errands, chat with other parents, or I took a nap. The higher up a player goes, the less a parent will likely attend practice. In college, parents are b-a-n-n-e-d.

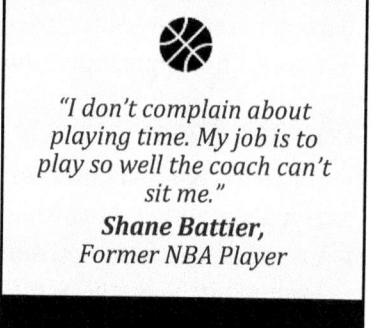

"I don't complain about playing time. My job is to play so well the coach can't sit me."
Shane Battier,
Former NBA Player

One day I had time to kill, so I stopped by a Morgan State practice. Until then, no one had ever told me parents were not allowed. When practice was over and the head coach and I exchanged greetings, he made a point of "nicely" remarking, "I almost put you out..."From that day forward, I understood the assignment.

Playing Time and the Sideline Engagers

Across America, the largest bleacher conversations are parents complaining about their son's playing time. As a parent, soliciting a coach for game time is one way to get under their skin.

A new trend is forming in youth basketball, and that is the idea of closed practices. Coaches are fed up with parent interference. Coaches are seemingly also tired of explaining that game time is based upon a player's performance in practice. It also can be used as a punishment for bad grades, being late to practice, a lack of sheer effort, among other reasons. I know parents who keep up with the exact number of minutes their son plays in every game. Watching your son sitting on the bench, more than playing, can be one of the most frustrating things parents have to deal with.

At the beginning of Chad's basketball life, I admit that the lack of playing time made me a little emotional. I fell in line like the other parents. Chad and I may have spoken about, but I would call a million other coaches or family members, before I would ever discuss it with his coach. My rationale is that parents should not have a say in a coach's decision inside the locker room or on the court. They will likely only tell you what you want to hear to get rid of you if you inquire.

I highly doubt a coach will ever put a player in the game due to pressure from a parent. Depending on the player's age, after you make your demand, that coach will likely crucify your son. At the next practice, your son may ask, "Why do we have to run an extra 30 minutes today?"

The coach: "Oh no, sir, *you* have 50 minutes today."

Parents can learn from players. When a coach keeps a player on the bench, what do they do? They sit quietly and stay ready to go in if they are called. They do not yell, scream, or throw tantrums. The reality is that only five players can get on the court at any time. If you want to know why your son has not played, ask him first. He probably was already been told why—he just kept it from you.

If your son is "excessively" sitting on the bench, which depreciates him as a basketball player, try investigating it with another member of the coaching staff. Start on a positive note. Let them know your son is playing basketball to have fun. You can point out that research reveals that 90% of children would rather play on a losing team than sit on the bench for a winning team.[25] Ask them the reason your son is not playing.

If it becomes a trend, that coach may not see value in your son. He may need individualized help, or he may be on the wrong team. It is that simple. The purpose is for your son to play, not sit it out, hoping to play someday. Remember, the basketball clock to college, or beyond, is still ticking.

Final Thoughts on Coaches

In a conversation with Ken Hoyte, Ph.D., a coach at Brooklyn Collegiate High School in New York City, we discussed honesty from coaches. I sought the rationale (and apprehension) in coaches providing their observation on a player's performance to parents. He shared,

> *"Very rarely will a coach tell a parent their child isn't good enough because most parents will believe the coach is a dream killer."*

To any coaches reading this, if you believe an athlete has potential, let a parent know. If you believe an athlete is high-level, admit that you have a gem. If you think there is still work to be done, share that. Let parents know how we can help. Many of us may even have resources that you likely can use.

Coaches, and handlers, should also know it is creepy and unorthodox for them to contact our minor children without our knowledge—especially during school hours or late at night. In particular, if they are a coach on a competing team. It causes some parents to change their son's phone number. Thankfully, I never had to do that, but I encourage parents to set up rules of engagement with their son. Make sure he communicates with you when any "adult" makes contact.

Youth basketball coaches are likely parents themselves, so they should understand that not all parents mean any disrespect or harm. Just like many of them, we are raising our children and want them to be treated like children, not adults before their time. Coaches are going to be a considerable influence during a critical development stage of their life so it should be a team effort to help them become successful.

Connecting the Dots

Yes, unruly parents may have made it challenging for coaches and parents to connect in meaningful ways.

Chad and I have a rule for coaches, teachers, and others in similar positions. Unless an adult crosses a line, which may harm him, he cannot complain to me about them while under their tutelage. It would be best if you did not allow it either.

If I left my son with a math tutor, I would not tell that tutor how to teach algebra. If my son is learning Spanish with a teacher who speaks fluent Spanish daily, I will not interrupt. Parents entrust a coach to "coach" our sons. We may know their talents, but it is best left to the professionals to define and refine them.

When Michael Jordan was in high school, he was placed on junior varsity over the varsity team. Jordan went to his mother, Deloris Jordan, to complain. She responded, "Work harder and get better so you can be on varsity next year."[26]

Great advice.

If there are complaints, you should follow the unspoken chain of command. Your son takes his grievances to his coach for a solution before involving you. On the other hand, there may be coaches who are not as welcoming, and your son may not feel there is an open-door policy for him (or his parents). That is a different issue. If this is true, you should know that your son is not a priority, nor should you have faith that the coach is the best fit for him.

Coaches and parents must devise a way to be more respectful because we both need one another, and young people are watching us.

If not, parents must trust their own process and do what they feel is best for their child.

Parent Suggestions to Coaches

Parents can make the following suggestions to a coach:

- Request they start the season with a parent meeting. At the meeting, they can share their mission and vision for the team, along with a written code of team ethics for players.
- Provide information on the best contact person on their staff for questions.
- Give parents a game and practice schedule at the start of the season.
- When traveling, share the hotel and transportation information.
- Let parents know what a player may need for away games.
- Let parents know if they can attend away games.
- Tell parents how to promote the team and support the sponsors.
- Ask parents what is needed from them financially and when.

Questions coaches can ask during their recruitment and registration process.

Some teams are organized well. Others could use administrative support. Not once have we ever received a recruitment, or a policy manual from any team. Coaches looked at, or heard about, my tall son who could hoop and said, "Let's go. Mom, we got him."

A few may have added, "Oh, can you sign this liability waiver?" If coaches were more forthcoming in the beginning, it could thwart potential issues and possibly help them with player selections.

Coaches can possibly ask parents to answer the following during recruitment/registration:

- What is the most important thing I need to know about your child?
- How are his grades in school? What would he like to be when he grows up?
- When was your son's last health physical, including a heart check?
- Is your son on any medication?
- Is there any part of the season your child will be out for any reason (school assignments, family vacations, etc.)?
- What are your child's strengths and weaknesses?
- What is the most important thing your child needs to develop, or learn, this year?
- Are you willing to work with your son outside of general practice time, or hire a personal trainer?
- What are your son's plans for their future, and how will you define success?
- Who is your son's emergency contact?
- What type of friends does he have and do you know them?

Where to Locate Information on Coaches

The following websites provide information on coaches at all levels, including their salaries:

- National Association of Coaches - nabc.org
- National Junior College Basketball Coaches Association (NJCBCA) – jcbca.weebly.com
- [College] Coaches Database – coachesdatabase.com

Referees/Officials

Referees are an extremely important part of youth basketball. They are the custodians of the game. They not only watch everything during a game, but are likely the ones who know what is going on in the stands of smaller gyms where most youth games are held. Their role is also to keep players safe on the court. Parents, who often see them as enemies, need to respect them. Parents yelling unkind words at them from the sidelines is terrible for the game.

Referees, who rarely interact with parents, are an underappreciated resource in youth basketball. I am amazed at the way they stay in such great shape, especially those who are middle-aged and are able to run up and down the court with kids.

Youth basketball referees may be volunteers, or they may only make $25 or $50 a game. College referees can earn up to $3,000 per game. In 2022, NBA referees' salaries were between $180,000 to $500,000.[27] Kenny "Coach Boobie" Jackson shared,

> ***"Many referees are former players and want to represent good basketball. Some also work in youth basketball to move up to the collegiate or professional levels."***

Therefore, I seriously doubt any of them have a personal vendetta against your son or his team. It would be best if parents refrained from screaming at them, as referees can remove any player, coach, or spectator. They can also end the game in a forfeiture.

In college and the pros, a player and a coach know the true power of referees who rarely hesitate to hand out technical fouls for infractions. Why is that lost in youth basketball?

It is so bad that Brian Barlow "publicly shames people who physically and verbally abuse sports officials." He also pays $100 for videos of irate people, and then uploads them to his Facebook page, @Youroffside, hoping to embarrass them.

Additionally, due to the verbal and even physical abuse of referees, the number of youth basketball referees is dwindling.

The National Association of Sports Officials (NASO) estimates that between 20%-25% of officials are expected never to come back post-pandemic. NASO also reports that since March 2020, their membership has declined from 29,000 to 23,000.[28]

Do we really want coaches scrambling for game coverage? Or worse, the reduction of youth basketball games? The only ones who will suffer are the players. Parents who want to act up should also remember that referees speak to coaches outside of the gym. They just may have the ear of one of the college coaches trying to recruit your son.

Dr. Martin Luther King, Jr. once said, "Nothing in all the world is more dangerous than sincere ignorance and conscientious stupidity." Word to the wise, please leave the referees alone and let them officiate the game in peace.

CHAPTER III

The Early Years & High School

"Mom and Dad, welcome to your biggest seasons."
—Simone Joye

The Early Years

Children can start learning the basics of basketball from kindergarten to third grade. However, both youth sports and child development experts acknowledge that 5-6-year-olds are not ready to play on a team. They also agree that kids are not ready for competition until they are at least eight years old.[29] Before then, they report children cannot handle the stresses of winning, losing, or being measured and scored on their performance.

"While many coaches will recommend that kids start playing at a younger age, there are benefits to starting at a later age. In fact, according to a study by the American Academy of Pediatrics, kids who start playing basketball in middle school or high school may actually have a lower risk of developing cardiovascular disease later in life."[30]

Parents should note that NCAA Division 1 (D1) and Division 2 (D2) college coaches are not allowed to initiate communication with recruits until June 15 after their sophomore year or September 1 of their junior year of high school. However, allegedly many coaches will make scholarship offers to student-athletes in the 7th and 8th grade.

Chad joined his first basketball team at the age of 6 after an AAU coach approached us in a store and shared the benefits of him playing.

He might have saw a future in basketball for him. I saw him staying active afterschool and on the weekends. I personally believe all young people should be allowed to participate in physical activity to counter the obesity crisis in America. Former First Lady Michelle Obama launched "Let's Move: America's Move to Raise a Healthier Generation of Kids" (Letsmove.gov) to "combat the epidemic of childhood obesity." It is also a great resource.

Although Chad played basketball in elementary school, he did not begin taking it "seriously" until the 8th grade. Had I known it would eventually be a career goal for him, I would have started letting him play on a regular basis earlier. It probably would have prevented his rocky start in high school.

High School Years

The high school years are the most critical years for a basketball player's development if they plan to play competitively at the next level.

A high school player will play about 80-140 games and they will need to make sure those games count. Parents of players who are pursuing college scholarships can expect to be busy during these years as you help prepare them for the next level.

In the United States, there are 540,800 male high school basketball players.
Source: NCAA.org

High school basketball time seems to go by at a warped speed, so do your best to also enjoy the games.

The most important day for a high school basketball player is the first time he suits up. Many parents hear all the time, "Do not worry, he still has time. "Do not believe it, and do not allow anyone to stall your son.

Once your son starts playing in high school, you can research the governance of high school basketball. One place to start is The National Federation of State High School Associations (NFHS), which makes the rules for high school sports, including basketball (nfhs.org).

If your son is planning to attend an NCAA D1 college, parents should also begin seeking guidance from coaches, guidance counselors, teachers, NCAA representatives, and other parents as soon as possible.

Academics as a Priority

NCAA leaders and our nation's legislators care greatly about prioritizing academics for all athletes. Many great high school players, who were fascinating on the court, have had their basketball futures end due to poor grades. Others are delayed, or weeded out, because they took the wrong classes or missed important deadlines.

> *Important for Parents*
> The NCAA has a "high school portal" where parents and players can register to view their approved high school courses from any American high school.
> You will need your son's NCAA High School code or CEEB/ACT code.

To help you organize, consider keeping a five-subject notebook or creating an electronic system for keeping notes and important deadlines. You will want to keep track of your son's grades each semester beginning in the 9th grade. You also want to ensure that any failed classes, or those with a D grade, are made up as soon as possible in the summer, during an intercession, or the following academic year.

If, for any reason, the classes cannot be made up at your son's school, there are online virtual high schools that are used by many athletes. One is the University of Nebraska Online High School (highschool.nebraska.edu). Credits from online virtual high schools are likely acceptable by your State Education Department and the NCAA.

The first thing a college coach will request is your son's transcript which is sent to their college compliance office to determine if they qualify for a scholarship. Navigating eligibility guidelines is not easy for the novice and it takes a significant amount of time. You can begin to

THE EARLY YEARS & HIGH SCHOOL

monitor compliance yourself with your son's grades using the NCAA eligibility checklist. You can download the fillable form from their website. There you will also be able to view the required classes and credit hours needed to help your son's school plan his courses. Although high school personnel will be responsible for this, trust then verify. Check, then double (and triple) check.

The NCAA has criteria which determines not only qualifications for scholarships, but the level in which an athlete can compete. Grades and your son's GPA will determine whether they can play at the D1, D2, or D3 level; whether they are a red-shirt; fully qualified, etc.

If your son is off the mark, and it is not recoverable, the college cannot offer them a scholarship.

Top academic areas to **PAY SPECIAL ATTENTION** to:

- The core classes and credits required to graduate from high school according to your State's Education Department and on the list of NCAA-approved high-school courses in the NCAA Eligibility Center. Visit ncaa.org and search: High school portal where you can check to ensure your son's class registrations are in alignment.

- The NCAA core-course GPA and the state's graduation GPA are likely two different numbers. The NCAA also denotes that a student-athlete must take certain classes within a specific timeframe. You can find more information in the *NCAA Guide for the College Bound Athletic*, a free publication published annually.

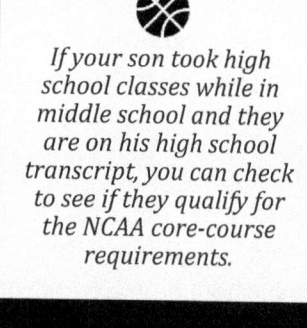

If your son took high school classes while in middle school and they are on his high school transcript, you can check to see if they qualify for the NCAA core-course requirements.

- The GPA needed to be admitted to a college per their admissions office. Your son may qualify to play basketball per the governing bodies, or even from the college's athletic department. You must also ensure he is eligible for college admittance from their admissions office. You can use the "GPA Calculator" at gpacalculator.net to find out the GPAs of the majority of U.S. Colleges and their SAT/ACT requirements.

The *US News & World Report* also publishes an annual report on colleges and acceptance criteria at usnews.com/best-colleges.

Grade by Grade

The 9th Grade and 10th grades are the years of accumulation in high school basketball. If your son is not an asset to the team, has a bad attitude, is late to practice, has poor grades, or is unmotivated, the likelihood of them advancing may be at risk. This is also the time to determine whether your son has any academic challenges and to begin working on them with his school's guidance counselor and teachers.

For example, does he need an Individual Education Plan (IEP)? Does he need additional resources to learn, such as an auditory aid or a tutor? If so, immediately work on obtaining academic support for him. Working on this early in high school can make a huge difference regarding college acceptance. This is also a good time for him to explore electives, such as music, art, and technology, to help balance his learning. However, be sure not to overload electives over core classes. Get the most important classes done early.

The 9th and 10th grades.

Begin connecting with college coaches: You and your son can contact a college coach at any time. Just be careful you follow the allowable timeline and rules for engagement. For example, if you call a coach he can answer, conversate, and ask for more information. He will not be able to call you back should he miss the call. Chapter V explains contact periods.

Prepare for the SAT/ACT: Although the NCAA is permanently banning standardized testing as a qualification to play in their member schools, you still may want your son to consider taking the SAT/ACT in the 9th or 10th grade. If he does not obtain an NCAA basketball scholarship, he may need his test scores for the NAIA, or to be admitted into college as a player, or a general student. You can find free, or low-cost, SAT/ACT prep courses, and practice tests, at The Princeton Review, The College Board, Khan Academy, or Kaplan. You can also check with local nonprofits in your area who may offer free help.

The Early Years & High School

Playing Summer Basketball: If your son has not yet played on an AAU, or another grassroots team, you should begin looking for a team in the winter of the 9th grade for the following spring. Grassroots recruitment and try-outs start near the end of the high school basketball season. These games are attended by many college coaches and are an excellent way for your son to compete with great players and get exposure. More on grassroots programs can be found in Chapter IV.

The 11th and 12th grade.

Check and make sure your son's classes and grades still match with governing body requirements. This is also the time when general high school students are heavily researching what their graduation options will be. Basketball players should do the same in the 11th grade.

In the 12th grade, students are preparing for prom, graduation, and yearbook photos. General students are receiving college acceptance letters. Some basketball players have already committed to college programs. If your son is still awaiting his celebration, this may be a tough time for him. It is also time to quickly find other options that you can read about in Chapter V under *No Scholarship Offer? It's Not Over.*

Homeschooled student-athletes

There is an overall increase in the number of homeschooled students, and that number surged during the pandemic. Student-athletes are opting to complete their high school education from the comfort of home, which allows them more time to practice their game.

Although the NCAA and the National Association of Intercollegiate Athletics (NAIA) allow student-athletes to be homeschooled, ten states do not allow them to participate in sports (California, Connecticut, Delaware, Maryland, Mississippi, Montana, New York, North Carolina, Oklahoma, and West Virginia).

Homeschooled students are still required to register in the NCAA Eligibility Center and meet the same standards as all other student-athletes. You can find more information on the NCAA website.

If you have a homeschooled student-athlete, or are considering it, check out the National Christian Homeschool Basketball Championship (NCHBC). Founded in 1991, the NCHBC runs the largest homeschool sporting event and has a wealth of information on homeschooled athletes. Their website is nchclive.com.

High School Equivalency Diploma (GED) may be accepted as proof of graduation under certain conditions. It will not satisfy the requirements for core courses, the core-course GPA, or SAT/ACT scores. It also may not be accepted by some four-year colleges. Student-athletes with a GED may want to consider a junior college (JUCO) as a viable option. Parents can contact the NCAA or NAIA Eligibility Centers to learn how to submit a GED as proof of graduation and applicable test scores.

The High School Difference: Public vs. Private Schools

Basketball has changed so much in the past few decades. During the 1960s and 1970s, more than 90% of NBA players were from urban communities and attended public schools. The average NBA salary back then was $35,000 a year. Today, over 100 players make that "per day."

From the 1990s into the 21st century, the educational institutions for high school basketball players shifted. In the 2019 NBA draft, 45% of the first-and-second round draftees attended private schools vs. 35% who attended public schools. What I also found is that those public schools were likely located in suburban communities.

Playing basketball in urban public high schools no longer seems to be the draw for college recruiters that it once was. Not many college recruiters are going "to the hood" for basketball players, even though they still may have some of the best coaches in youth basketball—coaches who have won state championships over private and parochial schools. However, their talent pool is shrinking, their players need more exposure, and the urban public schools need greater resources, facilities and funding to compete.

Dr. John Marschhausen, the Superintendent of Dublin City Schools (Ohio) states,

> *"We see them [public school athletes] coming out to a point, and then when they see that this isn't going to be an option, they quit. This is an uncomfortable issue for*

The Early Years & High School

> *us as a public school district to say we have kids who can't compete because of socioeconomics. The opportunity is there because they can tryout, but because they don't have the skills, it's a false sense of opportunity,"*[31]

If your son is playing in an urban public school and a private school is not an option, you should try your best to get him on a well-known AAU team, in basketball camps and academies as much as possible. These other options will help him get in front of college recruiters, as well as allow him to compete. This way when coaches come to watch others, they will also see your son. Many college recruits, and NBA prospects, have been discovered in this manner.

Catholic, Christian, and Prep High Schools

Catholic high schools have great basketball teams that compete in highly competitive conferences which are of interest to college coaches. According to the United States Conference of Catholic Bishops, there are approximately 1,205 Catholic high schools with an average tuition cost of $11,066.

Paolo Banchero (Orlando Magic), the number one NBA draft pick in 2022 attended O'Dea High School, a Catholic high school in downtown Seattle.

A few nationally ranked Catholic high school teams include:

- Archbishop Molloy (New York)
- Archbishop Stepinac (New York)
- Bishop Gorman (Nevada)
- Christ the King (New York)
- DeMatha Catholic High School (Maryland)
- Mater Dei (California)
- Notre Dame (California)
- Roselle Catholic (New Jersey)
- St. Paul VI (Virginia)

The following Christian high schools are considered powerhouses:

- Calvary Christian (Florida)
- Long Island Lutheran (New York)
- Modesto Christian (California)
- Our Saviour Lutheran (New York)
- St. Rita (Illinois)
- Sunrise Christian (Kansas)
- Word of God (North Carolina)

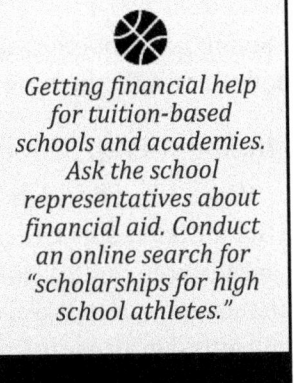

Getting financial help for tuition-based schools and academies. Ask the school representatives about financial aid. Conduct an online search for "scholarships for high school athletes."

Prep Schools

Prep schools (also known as boarding schools) are usually located in picturesque rural communities on sprawling campuses that can rival some college ones. Their tuition is comparable to colleges, and they offer financial assistance for basketball players.

Critics argue that instead of parents paying for prep school, those dollars should be used for college. That sounds good in theory, but basketball players who attend prep schools have multiple advantages over other high school students, including being academically prepared for college. Their classes are smaller and held in state-of-the-art classrooms with students and teachers from around the world. They are assets to college coaches because they believe students who attend them will have a higher probability of success when they arrive on their campus. Some of those coaches may even be alumni who attend games on campus, thereby giving prep school students greater access to them and their representatives. Even without basketball, prep school students have a greater chance of graduating and gaining entrance into some of the nation's best colleges.

Young players seem to enjoy the opportunity. The chance to leave home while in high school, live on a campus, have unlimited access to a gym, as well as travel is not something many high school players would decline.

Chad made the decision for himself to leave one of New York City's best basketball high schools to attend a prep school. He was awarded a

The Early Years & High School

generous financial package in exchange for his participation in their basketball program. He also had a coach who cared about him as a person, his academic studies, and his future on the court. I also slept better at night knowing he was safe at any moment of the day, or night.

Finding A Prep School

When Chad decided he wanted to attend prep school we began with a Google and a social media search. We returned emails from prep school coaches who had reached out to him, but most were in the Midwest or on the west coast. We also informed every coach we knew that Chad was interested in attending prep school. Coach Ken Hoyte, Ph.D., assisted and made phone introductions. He also took Chad and other players to visit several prep schools. Chad and I also hit the road and visited four schools.

For weeks, Chad had video interviews, met with school officials, and the basketball team. He completed applications and admission essays. We stayed overnight in hotels or had 12-hour days on the road. Some days, I was so tired I had to pull over and catch a nap at highway rest stops while Chad studied or worked on his current school assignments. It was a grueling two months before he aced his interview and was admitted to The MacDuffie School in Granby, MA under Coach Jacque Rivera.

Read the article by Rob Book:
"For many NBA players, finding a better high school was critical to success."
theconversation.com

Chad was lucky because Coach Rivera works for his players. He is a coach who will pick up the phone and work hard to get players a college scholarship. He was resourceful regarding parental guidance and is the one who gave me the most information on how parents participate in the college recruiting process.

Chad played great basketball and finished his senior year at MacDuffie and then went with Coach Rivera to do a post-grad year at the Woodstock Academy in Woodstock, CT.

That year, Coach Rivera graduated a blockbuster team at MacDuffie. Several went on to do big things in basketball, including James Bouknight (Charlotte Hornets), who went to play at UConn and was selected in the first round, 11th pick in the 2021 NBA draft; Ismael Massoud went to Wake Forest and now plays at Kansas State; and Richie Springs plays at UConn.

You should also be aware, depending upon the location, that prep school basketball may be divided by "classes," similar to college divisions. If you decide on the prep school route, make sure your son will be playing in the top class because this is where college coaches recruit from.

Instead of a prep school, another option may be the Hargrave Military Academy in Chatham, VA. Former NBA player Coach Larry Brown did a post-graduate year there. Brown is considered one of the NBA's greatest coaches and is the only basketball coach in history to win an NCAA national championship and an NBA title.

Finding the right prep school, if that is the route you would like to explore, is as arduous as deciding on a college, and so is the application process. Your son should reach out to a prep school coach the way he would to a college coach. You can visit Max Preps at maxpreps.com to find a list of prep schools. The Army and Navy Academy also wants parents to know they are "a hidden gem on the west coast" and since 1910, they have "been educating and developing future leaders and athletes through a rigorous college prep experience specifically built for boys in grades 7-12." Tuition there starts at $30,800 for day school and $52,800 for boarding school for both U.S. and international students. You can visit them at armyandnavyacademy.org.

Basketball Academies: Another High School Option

Cory Heitz has written an informative article, *"Prep Schools vs. Basketball Academies: What are the Differences and Why Does It Matter?"*

Heitz defines basketball academies as:

The Early Years & High School

> *"A program where a player can attend for a school year. These academies can be for a 9th-12th grader, while some are strictly for post-grads. A basketball academy focuses on basketball first and foremost. Some academies partner with a small Christian or private school for their player's schooling. The private school likes this because they receive tuition and potential notoriety. Some academies only have online learning as an option."*

You can read the full article on the PREP Athletics website at prepathletics.com. It is worth exploring to see if this could be an option, along with how to avoid rampant scams or other devious practices.

Basketball academy recruitment can come at any time. When Chad was in the 11th grade, we got a call from a school on the west coast. The coach discussed the benefits of Chad leaving Loughlin to attend his Academy. He said all of the right things, including his connections to college coaches and academic support for players. He was also willing to offer Chad a full scholarship. It sounded great, and Chad was interested.

Then two issues emerged. The first one was that the coach wanted to fly Chad out alone for a visit. The second was regarding housing. The coach shared, "The boys live in the house with me and my wife." There was no way my minor son would live in the personal space of a coach whom I had never met on the other side of the country.

A year later, they were flagged for issues regarding their academic accreditation.

I learned that basketball academies put the "athlete" before the student. I have no doubt Chad would have likely excelled on the court—but what about his academics?

Coaches may not realize it, but that question stays on the minds of many basketball parents, even if their son plays well. Parents should always think about what the plan will be when their son turns 18 years old and can no longer, or does not want to, play basketball. What happens to the basketball prodigy whose grades prevent him from obtaining a college scholarship? Will he go to college, the military, or a trade school? What about the player who makes it to the pros and earns an astronomical salary, but academics may have never been a priority in his household growing up?

Professional athletes lose a lot of money to fraud. From 2014 to 2018, Ernst & Young estimates that professional basketball players lost over $100 million to fraud.[32] And that was data from players who were not too embarrassed to report it. Could their failure to have financial literacy be blamed on coaches and parents willing to pass young players through?

Basketball Academies

In my opinion, the undeniable basketball academy leader is IMG Academy in Bradenton, FL, where tuition is $87,900 per year. IMG also offers one-week and three-week camps, with fees from $1,999 to $9,159.

Their website at imgacademy.com states," IMG Academy is the world's most prestigious sports, performance, and educational institution. Established in 1978 with a pioneering concept known as the Nick Bollettieri Tennis Academy, IMG Academy has grown to become a global phenomenon." Their alumni include Jaden Springer (Philadelphia 76ers), Dwight Powell (Dallas Mavericks), and Kenyon Martin Jr. (Houston Rockets).

The IMG campus looks like a tropical resort. They seem to have every amenity possible for student-athletes and their families including their own luxury accommodations, The Legacy Hotel at IMG Academy.

It is one of those places you look at as a basketball parent and know that your son would be in great hands. Even in my conversations with their admissions staff, they always put the student-athlete first.

Great

Honorable mentions of other popular basketball academies:

The Spire Academy (Ohio)
Hillcrest Prep Academy (Arizona)
Link Academy (Missouri)
Oak Hill Academy (Virginia)

Reclassification

Reclassification is not new and reclassifying students for kindergarten has been studied for decades. A parent may delay a child from starting school to allow them extra time to mature cognitively or socially. Students may also be skipped to a higher grade based upon their academic achievements.

In basketball, reclassification, also known as reclassifying or reclassing, is to change a player's basketball high school graduation date. A player can reclassify "up" as in the case of Karl Anthony Towns (Minnesota Timberwolves), Andre Drummond (Chicago Bulls), and Andrew Wiggins (Golden State Warriors), which allowed them to play in college sooner and enter the NBA draft a year earlier.

However, most references to basketball reclassification have players going the opposite direction." Some also reference it as, "Staying back to get ahead."

According to the Student-Athlete Academy, a basketball program for students in grades 7 and 8 in Wyckoff, NJ, reclassed students also "might have a late birth date for his/her sport.

Reclassifying: One year Better but One Year Behind, by Garland Cooper, defines it as:

> *"When a student-athlete and their parents make a conscious choice to be "held back" in high school, (and in some states, as early as middle school). It's registering with a graduating class later than your original, with the intention of developing better grades and test scores. And, from a sports perspective, giving the student-athlete another year to get bigger, stronger, taller, and more mature."*[33]

Cooper also notes that "Reclassifying is tougher than you think. It's complicated." He shares, "Making the wrong move at the wrong time could adversely affect not only your child's college eligibility but their high school eligibility as well."

Tony Hargraves, a former head coach and the current program director for the Riverside Hawks in New York City, who played basketball at Iona College shared, "When you reclassify a student, parents will need to find another school."

Hargraves also said parents should know,

> *"Parents have to set realistic goals. I am not trying to be a dream killer. Parents have to think carefully about reclassifying because it can backfire. If my son is only 5'10" and never made an All-state or All-city team, there may be some misplaced value for leaving him a grade behind and paying thousands of dollars in tuition to prep schools."*

When reclassifying works well, Hargraves admits, "Propelling forward can be tremendous."

Parents and players must also be careful about transferring within public school districts for basketball. Public schools do not allow reclassification, and reclassed students usually end up at a prep school or a basketball academy. Parents will need to find out your State Education Department's transfer rules because some may require a player to sit-out a year. California education officials are monitoring parents who are transferring basketball students based upon "moving to a new address."

However, Attorney Michelle Ball, notes in her blog post (edlaw4students.com), *"Improved, But Still Confusing CIF High School Sports Transfer Rules,* that "a student who moves, can seek a hardship waiver."

If you are a parent considering reclassifying your son, some believe it is best to do it before high school.

Post-Graduate Year

A post-graduate (or post-grad) year immediately follows high school graduation. A player spends a year in a prep school, or at a basketball academy instead of going straight to college. The post-grad year seeks to help improve their academic and/or basketball skills. It works for a student-athlete who may not have qualified for full eligibility due to their grades. Some players with college offers also may decide on the post-grad route to see if their "stock" goes up to secure higher level college offers.

A post-grad year is also considered a better option for players than going the D2 or the JUCO route because it will not count against their playing time in college. It is also a viable option for a high school senior who was not recruited, or lacks any scholarship offers.

National High School Basketball Tournaments

It may be beneficial if your son is on a team that plays in any of the following tournaments. It would guarantee that he will be seen by college coaches and afford him opportunities to compete with highly skilled talent. You can inquire with your son's coach as to whether he is familiar with them or seek a team for him that will participate in at least one.

- Adidas National Tournament (various locations)
- All the Smoke Classic (Arizona)
- Barry Pruitt Hurricane Classic (Arkansas)
- Bass Pro Shop Tournament of Champions (Missouri)
- Chicago Elite Classic (Illinois)
- Dick's High School National Tournament (NYC)
- Geico Nationals (Florida)
- Holiday Hoopsgiving (Georgia)
- Kevin Brown Memorial Tournament of Champions (Illinois)
- National High School Invitational (various locations)
- NorCal Tip Off Classic (Connecticut)
- Spaulding Hoophall Classic (Springfield, MA)
- Tarkanian Classic (Las Vegas)
- Thanksgiving Hoopfest (Texas)
- The Les Schwab Invitational (Oregon)

High School Basketball Fun Facts

- There are typically 20-35 high school games per season.
- The season usually lasts 5 months (September to March/April).
- A game is four 8-minute quarters.
- Overtime is four minutes.
- There are no replays in high school basketball.
- Most high schools do not use shot clocks. Only eight states previously used them, although the NFHS has mandated that they are now allowed in every state starting in the 2022-23 season.[34]
- The size of the boys' team basketball: 29.5 inches
- The coaching box (28 feet) is smaller than in college (38 feet).
- Home jerseys must be white. Away games use dark jerseys.
- Jersey numbers range from 00 to 15, 20 to 25, 30 to 35, 40 to 55, and 50 to 55.
- Headgear for medical or religious reasons are allowed with documented proof that must be shared with officials at each game.

CHAPTER IV

The Other Seasons: Grassroots & AAU

"Talent is insignificant. I know a lot of talented ruins. Beyond talent lie all the usual words: discipline, love, luck, but most of all endurance."

— James Baldwin (1924-1987)

Basketball has become a year-round sport. In addition to the school season, much of youth basketball also occurs through other programs known as grassroots (or travel) basketball. These programs occur primarily in the early spring through the summer. There are also fall leagues.

Grassroots basketball is a complex ecosystem run by independent operators. They can be either be immensely highly profitable programs or struggling for funding to cover the basics. All teams seem share a similar goal besides making money: to showcase basketball talent and provide a player pipeline for college and the professional leagues. Players compete in front of college recruiters, sponsors, scouts, parents,

THE OTHER SEASONS: GRASSROOTS & AAU

celebrities, and professional players. Quite a few teams provide wraparound comprehensive services including tutoring, life skills, and financial literacy.

The **Grassroots Basketball Association** (@tgbassociation), formed in 2020, currently promotes grassroots tournaments from around the nation.

The **National Basketball Players Association** (NBPA) (nbpa.com) has a grassroots program which "consists of innovative, live and online basketball and life skill development experiences, designed for youth to learn, have fun, and maximize their potential, both on and off the court."

The **AAU** (Amateur Athletic Union) is considered to have the premier grassroots basketball program. AAU teams on "the circuit" are some of the most sought-after by young hoopers.

Troy Moses, a former player at Ball State currently playing for Lusitania in Portugal, shared his benefit:

> *"I had no offers from high school basketball.*
> *[G]ot 12 Division 1 offers in one month from AAU."*

Founded in 1888, the AAU, headquartered in Orlando, FL, is a nonprofit with 700,000 members and 40+ sports programs. In 2020, their annual operating revenue was $10.1 million.

The mission of the AAU is "To offer amateur sports programs through a volunteer base for all people to have the physical, mental, and moral development of amateur athletes and to promote good sportsmanship and good citizenship." Their motto is "Sports for All, Forever."

The AAU defines boys & girls basketball teams by age levels: 13U, 14U, 15U, etc. (The "U" means under). Reclassification allows an older player to play on a team with younger players. It is not surprising to find a 16-year-old playing on the 15U team. Reclassification "up" means a 13-year-old player may play on a 14U team.

The AAU circuit is played from March through July. AAU games are serious travel events, not only for the players and coaches, but for photographers, videographers, members of the press, sponsors, and

The Parent's Section: Outside The Locker Room

fans of youth basketball. For sponsored team events, admission costs vary from free to $20+ per entry. Children under 5 are often free. For non-sponsored teams, tickets can cost up to $100 for a 2-day tournament. The sponsored national tournaments spare no expense for the multi-day events.

Imagine a super-sized state-of-the-art facility with multiple courts. Several games are being played simultaneously to standing room, wall-to-wall crowds with hundreds of people. The sounds from whistles, buzzers and PA announcements are loud. The pounding of the basketball hitting the gym floor is mixed with the sound of squeaking sneakers. Every few minutes, you will hear gasps and cheers from the crowd because a player has done something spectacular, or a team has won a game. Sponsor banners and player freebies are plentiful. Camera people and commentators are everywhere. There is reserved seating for too many college coaches to count. Player amenities include barbers, physical therapists, cryotherapy machines, green rooms, and photoshoots. Paramedics and security are on standby. Attendees include some of the best sports personnel in the nation.

College and prep school coaches, scouts, including NBA scouts, and corporate executives are walking around going nonstop on their phones. They are there to watch games hoping to find the next superstar or brand ambassador. You may also find a Hollywood celebrity there to support a family member playing. And there is no shortage of NBA players in attendance who may be watching their own children play. There are no autograph requests, or noticeable bodyguards. AAU coaches are having team meetings all over the facility.

As for college and prep school coaches, they are at a serious working recruitment event. They are critiquing players and taking notes in their guarded "coaches-only" pre-printed player programs which provide player information. Members of the media also receive their own versions as well.

Organizations are battling for the win, but also continued sponsorships from big brands. Players are not allowed to receive compensation of substantial value. Championship winners receive a

THE OTHER SEASONS: GRASSROOTS & AAU

trophy, a championship T-shirt, a hat, a backpack and the organization will receive a championship banner.

Playing on an AAU team can boost a young player's ego into the stratosphere. It is where most youth basketball players become well-known. Many of them are "branded" while playing. They receive professional photographs, are captured in excellent video footage, gain social media accolades, are interviewed by reporters, and younger players look up to them. Others may become a poster child for their team. John Lucas, the number one draft pick in 1976, who runs a basketball training center in Houston, explained the impact:

> *"They've been treated like they were a star since AAU in the 10th grade."*[35]

The young players who have been selected to play have connected with the right teams. They have arrived, some by private chartered jets, and are ready to show the nation's basketball leaders what they are capable of.

Their basketball futures may be at stake. A popular description of an AAU game is that it is "a place where a player gets exposure, or they get exposed." All players must bring their A-game. If they do not add value, they will not play. If they cannot play well, it will be seen quickly. It is one thing to be a talented player in their own town, city, or even state. When a player is on the AAU circuit and playing against players from across the nation, they had better bring it in beast mode, or they will be annihilated.

I have learned that many college coaches have little, if any, interest in the "show biz" side that has attached itself onto grassroots basketball. Parents should remember that formula and keep your son humble. Many AAU superstars age out, and they were never heard from again.

The average parent does not have a role at AAU tournaments. Most are surveying the room to see what college coaches are watching their son. They are hoping they will leave with a huge benefit—a verbal college offer. No parent is acting unruly. Nor are any yelling or screaming at their son on the court. Most are so quiet you may forget they are also in attendance.

The Parent's Section: Outside The Locker Room

At the Nike EYBL tournament I attended in 2019, mothers did receive an EYBL T-Shirt with the words, EYBL Mom on the front. On the back are the words, Love, Support, Time, Patience, & Sacrifice.

Parents may barely have time to speak with their son until they arrive back at the event's designated hotel. Parents also hang out and mingle at the hotel's bar. You might be invited to a game of spades or bid whist while parents happily talk about teams, coaches, and players. Other than that, parents, family, and friends who attend should have fun and lend support to their player and his team. If your son's team lost, you will likely still be packing in your hotel room while they are already on their way home. They move them in, and they move them out. In addition, you want to get a head start to the airport. After any large basketball event— from AAU tournaments to the All-Star game—the airport crowds and getting out of a host city is a noteworthy journalism feature.

Sponsored vs. Non-Sponsored Teams

The top three sponsors of AAU teams are Nike, Adidas, and Under Armour. In exchange for promotional opportunities, brand loyalty, and an investment in young people, they provide funding to AAU and other grassroots teams. As a result, players receive AAU membership, high-quality uniforms, playing sneakers, and all travel expenses, including meals.

The Largest AAU Tournaments

The AAU World Tournament, formerly as the AAU National Tournament, is a global event showcasing the top AAU teams from around the world. According to an AAU press release (June 21, 2022), there were an estimated 400 boys basketball teams. The 2023 championship games will be held at the ESPN Wide World of Sports Complex in Orlando, FL.

Nike EYBL (Elite Youth Basketball League) —Their championship game, the "Peach Jam" is played in late July in North Augusta, GA at the 120,000 square-foot Riverview Park Activities Center. In 2022, attendance was estimated at nearly 7,000, and it was projected to generate $6 million -$12 million in revenue for the city.[36] NBA Player's

EYBL teams include (or have included): Carmelo Anthony (Team Melo), Chris Paul (Team CP3), Kevin Durant (Team Durant), Russell Westbrook (Team Why Not), and Bradley Beal (Bradley Beal Elite).

Adidas Gauntlet Gold tournaments rotate in various cities, including Atlanta, GA, Charlotte, NC, and Seal Beach, CA. Their mission is, "Each summer Adidas provides a platform for tomorrow's basketball stars to develop their game and improve their skills."

NBA Player's Adidas Gauntlet teams include (or have included): James Harden (Team Harden), Damian Lillard (Team Lillard), Derrick Rose (Team Rose), Kyle Lowry (K-Low Elite), and John Wall (Team Wall).

Under Armour (UAA) rotate in various cities, including Carterville, GA, Mesa, AZ, Rock Hill, SC, and Bedford Park, IL. UAA states their goal is, "To offer boys and girls the opportunity to not only improve but also showcase skills and talents en route to their dreams of playing in college."

NBA Player's Under Armour Next Circuit teams include (or have included): Stephen Curry (Team Curry), Emmanuel Mudiay (Mudiay Elite), Raymond Felton (Team Felton), Will Barton (Team Thrill), Thaddeus Young (Team Thad), DeMarre Carroll (Team Carroll), Zach LaVine (Team Zach LaVine), Kevon Looney (Kevon Looney Elite), and Chuck Hayes (Chuck Hayes Basketball).

Non-Sponsored Grassroots Teams

An organization can have both sponsored and non-sponsored teams. For example, Nike may sponsor the 16U team but not the 15U. If your son is going to an AAU team, ask whether the team is sponsored.

Non-sponsored teams often struggle financially, and the expenses may be covered personally by the coach. Parents may be asked to cover their son's registration, uniforms, and travel. Parents have shared that the costs could be $2,000-$5,000 annually in some locations. Non-sponsored teams also have tournaments attended primarily by coaches from D2, D3, or JUCOs, which is still a plus for players.

The Parent's Section: Outside The Locker Room

Loyalty is Still a Virtue

> *"Over the years, AAU basketball has evolved from an organization dedicated to providing an outlet for children to improve skills and develop valuable skills such as teamwork and leadership to an industry designed to put money into its leaders pockets. The steady evolution has left AAU basketball in the hands of sleazy, money-hungry businessmen rather than conscientious adults with the kids' best interests at heart."*[37]
>
> Jay King, Lead Reporter
> covering the Boston Celtics for The Athletic

Although I believe most coaches, and owners of AAU teams, are good people, I have to agree with King, because there are quite a few who lack common decency.

Kenny "Coach Boobie" Jackson warns:

> *"Ninety percent of people in this business have an agenda. Ten percent have good intentions. Out of that 90%, there are 85% who have a hidden agenda—and that is dangerous."*

Chad has had his share of AAU adversity. His story is being shared so other parents can watch out and hopefully make better decisions than we did.

Chad started AAU on a non-sponsored team. Like many other players, he wanted to get a shot at a sponsored team. He finally got the opportunity and landed on a team that was 100 miles (roundtrip) from our home.

During the two years he played with them, his game improved, and other sponsored teams tried to recruit him. A coach we trusted said it was best not to move from team to team. My common sense should have prevailed. Professional players get traded to other teams all the time. There are players who are also free agents. There is a transfer portal for college players.

The Other Seasons: Grassroots & AAU

During Chad's second year, after a hard-fought battle where everyone on the team contributed, his team made it to the finals. One of his former AAU teams picked up a sponsorship after he left, and they had made it to the finals as well. Their coach called Chad and told him he wanted him to be the starting center, and that it was time for him "to come home." Although Chad was not a starter, he did not want to leave his current team. He seemed content, and he was playing fairly well. He also liked his coaches and teammates. There were no problems that I knew of, and the coaches were extremely helpful with the coordination of getting him to and from practice and games.

Two weeks before the finals were held, Chad did not know his travel information. I reached out to the "hands-on" team owner and was informed that Chad would not be playing in the finals with them. Instead, he was scheduled to play with the "B" team (that I did not even know existed) at a regional tournament in Pennsylvania. Just like that, Chad was replaced by another player, who I learned was selected because he had a large social media following. Allegedly, Chad's low social media presence was the deciding factor—not how he performed on the court. The "adults" who managed and coached the team allegedly felt the other player would garner them more financial opportunities through publicity on the national stage. Whatever the truth was, it was too late for Chad to go to the finals with his "come home" team.

One of the things I like about Chad is that he does not chase social media to validate him. He also knows many social media basketball stars who fizzled on the court, or in the eyes of coaches, because they wanted to be famous. Although the camera people seem to love him, as evidenced by all the press he has received, Chad is an introvert and is not a fan of the limelight. It is no coincidence that one of his favorite players, besides Derrick Rose (he would kill me if I did not mention him), is the reserved and quiet superstar Kawhi Leonard. Leonard is so reserved that his Twitter account, with over 500,000 followers, has three tweets and one retweet posted in 2015.

That summer, I refused to let Chad play on anyone's backup team after he had committed countless hours and worked so hard to be on the "A" team. It is these types of setbacks that can break a young player's spirit. I got the sense Chad began to believe he was not good enough for a national stage.

After I dried the private tears I had for my son, I got it together and thought to myself, it's just business. It was clear they wanted Chad to quit, nothing personal. Just another way to add to the attrition rates of players who give up and do not make it to the collegiate level. To this day, I still wonder, had I not called, when were they going to share the news with Chad? Were they going to embarrass him by sharing it in front of his teammates at practice?

Two years. One week before the finals he helped his team get to. It is not only what they did but how it was done. A parent cannot assume anything. I started looking for disappointments so regularly that wins seemed surreal.

Incidentally, his "come home" team beat the disloyal team at those *same* finals.

Chad had one year of AAU eligibility left, and he had yet to determine a new team. His "come home" team was not sponsored for the next age group so that meant they would not qualify to get to the national finals in next year. His dream of playing at a national AAU event was drifting away and it was a gloomy time. We pretty much focused on it for weeks.

They say, "Every exit is an entrance to someplace else." I hope all basketball parents remember that whenever your son may depart from a team—voluntarily or otherwise.

The next school year, Chad started at MacDuffie and Coach Rivera got him a try-out with the Boston-based Nike EYBL team, Expressions Elite XX. Chad always reminds me of something I told him long ago, "You said the storm comes before the shine."

He made the team and we celebrated. Once again, the sun came out for him and he did well on that national stage.

Chad joined a team loaded with awesome players including Bensley Joseph (University of Miami), Moussa Cisse (Oklahoma State), Dyondre

The Other Seasons: Grassroots & AAU

Dominquez (UMass) and the late Terrance Clark (University of Kentucky), who sadly passed away in 2021 in a car accident, just weeks before he would have been drafted. Terrance was a phenomenal young man and player. Chad still misses him.

Ironically, the first time a media company ever filmed me and posted the footage of me excited at a game, it was not even for Chad. Terrance did an explosive dunk at Peach Jam, and I jumped to my feet and screamed! That is the type of player he was, and I will never forget him. I pray that his family is well.

The Expressions' head coach, Todd Quarles, and his team (along with Coach Rivera once again) brought true happiness to my son and changed the game for him.

The XX family gave Chad a huge shot and treated him like the skillful player that he is. They ensured he was taken care of, on and off the court. Coaches and parent volunteers helped us with transportation to practices and local games in Boston. Coach Dexter Foy (Thank you!) let Chad stay in his home many nights when it was just not feasible for him to travel home to New York City due to inclement weather or otherwise.

They still support his efforts and are there for Chad as if he was adopted into a fraternity. As I began to think no one in youth basketball cared anything about the kids, the XX family and the "come home" team showed us what all youth basketball programs should aspire to. These are the types of team leaders parents should try and find for their son because when it works correctly, it can be a tremendous personal achievement for them.

They are out there, and the youth basketball industry could not run without them.

How to Find a Grassroots team, including AAU teams

- Request your son's high school coach reach out and contact AAU coaches.
- Your son can contact coaches himself and share his highlight video.

- Use the Club Locator tool on the AAU.com website. Many teams also list their tryout dates.

- Visit the top three sponsored team websites:

    Nike EYBL – nikeeyb.com
    Under Armour Next – underamournext.com
    Adidas Gauntlet – adidasgauntlet.com

The more teams you reach out to, the likelihood that your son will get selected. Grassroots coaches are always interested in meeting valuable players.

Final Grassroots/AAU Thoughts

- It is important to emphasize that parents should never accept any financial reward for their son to play basketball. If caught, your son will lose his eligibility to play in high school or college.

- It is great when any grassroots/AAU coach states he can obtain a scholarship for your son. If he is not a college coach who can make an actual offer, thank them, take it with a grain of salt, and do not depend on it as the only option.

- Grassroots basketball is a huge commitment. Make sure the team is flexible if your son needs to take end-of-year exams and/or needs to attend summer school.

- If your son plays for AAU, do not plan any vacations from March through July.

- If you are charged a registration fee, ensure the team is not "over stacking" the roster. Some organizations will take as many players as possible to get money, while the coach has no intention of allowing them to play.

THE OTHER SEASONS: GRASSROOTS & AAU

Basketball Camps

There is no substitute for playing basketball with live bodies.

Basketball camps help young people learn the game of basketball and provide individual evaluations. Camps are held for a few hours, or over a few days. Camps have both inexperienced and experienced players, so do not be surprised if some are more skillful than others. Basketball camps are also attended by college, AAU, and other grassroots coaches.

Types of Basketball Camps

- **Elite** basketball camps include college camps. They are usually during "live" periods from April – July. When a player visits a college camp (on a campus), it does not count towards their official and unofficial college visits covered in Chapter V.

- **Scouting/Evaluation/Exposure** camps are conducted by private organizations, such as nonprofits. Players invited to compete are not only evaluated, but possibly "ranked" for online scouting reports.

- **Development** camps are year-round programs to help a player elevate their game. These camps may also conduct workshops and other classroom training on basketball fundamentals.

If there are no basketball camps in your area, you may have to travel to one of the top cities for college basketball recruits. (View the list on page 101).

Elite Camps and Programs

- ***Allen Iverson RoundBall Classic***, co-founded by Bobby Bates, the Classic is one of youth basketball's most anticipated events and takes place in Memphis each April. It showcases 24 top high school seniors ranked in the Top 50. Iverson is hands-on with recruitment and the selection of players.

- ***The Black Student-Athlete Summit*** states that they are "the only event that caters to the holistic development of the Black Student-Athlete."[38] Founded by Leonard N. Moore, the Summit is held each May. Moore created the Summit while he was a Ph.D. student at Ohio State. Their goal "is to empower Black Student-Athletes to maximize their college experience by killin' it in the classroom and to not leave 'any meat on the bone' in terms of opportunities."

- ***Deaf Basketball Camps*** by the United States Association of America Deaf Basketball (USADF) provide opportunities for deaf and hard-of-hearing athletes. There is also the USA Deaf Sports Foundation (USADB).

- ***McDonald's All-American*** is an annual high school All-Star game that includes 24 players who are considered the top high school basketball players in the USA or Canada. Proceeds benefit the Ronald McDonald House charitable programs.

- ***National Wheelchair Basketball Association*** provides qualified individuals with physical disabilities the opportunity to play, learn, and compete.

- ***NCAA Elite Student-Athlete Symposium*** is conducted each September. According to the NCAA, this invitation-only event "provides high-profile college basketball athletes with information and networks to help them make decisions and understand issues surrounding a professional basketball career." The program is for student-athletes with a high probability of being drafted into the NBA, or an international league, who still have collegiate eligibility for the upcoming season.

- ***NCAA College Basketball Academy*** is held in several regions across the country. Players, who are registered in the NCAA Eligibility Center, can self-nominate themselves and are selected by college basketball head coaches and scouting agencies. The NCAA pays all expenses for the player and one parent to attend, including transportation, hotel accommodations and meals. A huge benefit was that they did more than the standard measurement of a player's height and weight. They tested Chad's vertical jump and measured his wing span. That become highly useful information that he shared with college coaches. Parents were also invited to an informative parent workshop to dialogue with NCAA, NBA, and NBPA executives. It was the first, and only, workshop on college recruitment I was ever invited to as a parent of a young basketball player. I am assuming it was the case for many others because at the conclusion the speakers

The Other Seasons: Grassroots & AAU

received thunderous applause. On Twitter, you can find them @TheCBBAcademy, and their website is thecbbacademy.com.

- **Nike Hoop Summit**, conducted every April, is considered one of the nation's premiere annual basketball tournaments. The Summit features America's top male high school seniors taking on a World Select Team comprised of top players, 19 years old or younger from around the world.

- **Pangos-All American Camp** created by Dinos Trigonis, is for hundreds of top high school players who, according to their website (pangosaacamp.com), "showcase their skills and talent in front of national scouts, media and video outlets." They also state, "It has become one of the top non-shoe affiliated grassroots basketball events in the country." Pangos is held each August in Long Beach, CA.

- **The Reno Memorial Basketball Tournament** for 4th-7th graders is considered the largest basketball tournament in the world. Hosted by Jam On it, they advertise the tournament as "a must attend event with over 1000 amateur youth teams participating."

- **Under Armour Elite 24** – Twenty-four of the country's elite high school players are selected for this tournament.

Taking It to The Street(Ball)

Streetball started in the early 1900s in Washington D.C. and New York City. Due to American segregation, it was created primarily for basketball players who were never given the opportunity to showcase their talents to professional scouts to become a professional basketball player."[39]

In the mid-1940s, Holcombe Rucker, a Black teacher and playground director for the New York City Parks Department, created outdoor basketball in Harlem that remains a summer ritual and a major part of youth and non-professional adult basketball. If your son is interested in participating in streetball tournaments, here are a few resources:

- **The Street Basketball Association** (sba.glo-impact.com), led by Jerrod Mustaf, was founded in 2001. Their mission is "To create a professional street basketball league and a forum for talented players to showcase their innovative and unique skills in front of television viewers and live audiences around the globe." Their catchy motto is, "We Got Our Five...Get Yours!"

Omari White has compiled a list entitled *The Most Notable Streetball Tournaments* located at one37pm.com, and it includes the following:

- Entertainers 155 **Rucker Park** Summer Classic New York, NY (Harlem). You can also find a list of Rucker Legends at nycstreetball.weebly.com. Since the 1960s, almost every basketball legend has played on the Rucker Court. The player's stories are fascinating and will likely be of huge interest to any young basketball player who also has access to play on those legendary courts.
- Kenny Graham's **West 4th Street** (The Cage) Pro-Am Classic, New York City (Greenwich Village)
- *Dyckman* Basketball League, New York City (Inwood)
- *Drew League*, Los Angeles, CA
- *George Goodman League*, Washington, D.C.
- *Crawsover* Pro-Am League, Seattle, Washington
- *Miami Pro-Am* Basketball League, Miami, FL

An honorable mention goes to the (Brand Jordan) **Quai 54**—which takes place in Paris, and is called the world's biggest streetball tournament. The organizers refer to it as "The Official Rendez-Vous of Basketball & Hip-Hop Culture." Breathtaking game photos under the Eiffel Tower can be found on their Instagram account @quai54wsc | website: quai54.com. There is also a Quai 54 Air Jordan brand sneaker.

Personal Training and Personal Coaches

Although players workout with their teams, they need someone to work with one-on-one. Trainers, or a personal coach, will get a player better physically and mentally, as well as quickly assess any deficiencies they may have. It is important you find one for your son if basketball is a serious endeavor.

Basketball great Bill Russell once said, "Concentration and mental toughness are the margins of victory." A basketball trainer, who is easy to find, will teach that.

One of my favorites is **David Zenon** (Instagram: @DaveZenon).

David, based in the New York City area, is a consummate professional who cares deeply about player development and young people. David could boast about his experience but chooses gratitude. I love his pinned Tweet he posted in 2018:

"5 years ago [2013] I had $5 to my name. I used that $5 to put gas in my car to train a kid. His family introduced me to very important people. It led to today where I get to workout guys like Mason Plumlee, Serge Ibaka, and other NBA players. Thank you to everyone who gave me a shot."

A favorite of many young players is New Jersey-based **Micah Lancaster** (Instagram: @micah_lancaster), who also appeared in the movie *Hustle*. Lancaster states in his Instagram bio, "100 NBA Players Trained" and "Travel to Train w/Me."

You can also find trainers on CoachTube.com, where there is a list of *"56 Great Basketball Coaches and Trainers to follow on Twitter."*

Avoiding Scammers

Reputable coaches warn parents about paying excessive fees for basketball services. Social media is filled with parents who share how they were duped. They say they have spent thousands of dollars on non-educational basketball activities without garnering any tangible results. When coaches or trainers want to work with your son or a school wants your son to play for them, the costs, if any, will be nominal.

You can also gauge how well your son plays through how much you are being charged for services. Think about how celebrities are offered so much for free, even though they likely can afford to pay. It is the same way in the business of youth basketball.

The Parent's Section: Outside The Locker Room

My motto is:

"The more you pay, the further away..."

The goal is to put your son in a position to be wanted and to ascertain where it is best to invest your money. For me, it has always been education. I let basketball take care of itself. I would not have paid thousands of dollars to a private basketball organization, an individual, or a basketball camp that could not grant high school or college credits.

NBA players who are the top in the field do not charge exorbitant fees for their camps or programs. Why should anyone else? Especially those which have been formed as a nonprofit charitable organization.

Parents also publicly share the benefits of their contributions. Their son's game may be improving, and he is playing regularly. He is forming new friendships, staying out of trouble, and is happy.

Unfortunately, greed has taken over, and parents are being taken advantage of. Most are paying for experiences that may lead to a dead end.

When Elon Musk became the owner of Twitter, he decided to charge for a blue checkmark verification. A baseball coach tweeted that Musk should set up a direct message system and "charge a fee" to contact people. He added, "You'd make a killing with college recruits wanting to reach college coaches." Great! Another way to hit parent's pockets. Someone seems to be always plotting on sports parents.

How can parents counter this in youth basketball? You can get your son's skill level assessed by an expert. If he is not getting the looks you feel he deserves, or you want to know the possibilities, you can invest in a legitimate college summer basketball camp. You can also consider a basketball training facility such as the one run by John Lucas in Houston, TX. You can view his website at johnlucasenterprises.com. The travel and registration fees will likely save you thousands of dollars in the long run.

The Other Seasons: Grassroots & AAU

If your son can play well, has the potential to be great, and/or is an anomaly, such as being taller than 6'6" (the average D1 basketball player's height), he already has a viable shot at a college scholarship.

There are great people in the youth basketball world who will help you and your son for free, or at a low cost. Pay for what you can afford, shop around, and obtain references whenever possible.

CHAPTER V

College Recruitment & Scholarships

"Parents spend thousands of dollars, (maybe tens of thousands, maybe more) on their kid's athletic pursuits to earn a college scholarship."

— Nick Buonocore, Founder, Reformed Sports Project

Playing sports is a pathway to a free college education. In youth basketball, obtaining a college scholarship is an important endeavor for many players and their parents. The unfortunate reality is that there are not enough of them for everyone.

USA Today High School Sports reports:

"It's a process with the potential to be worth hundreds of thousands of dollars in scholarship money — or to be an expensive lesson in dashed dreams."[40]

COLLEGE RECRUITMENT & SCHOLARSHIPS

If you conduct an online search, "How to get a college basketball scholarship?" you will find a plethora of information. Many resources are shared by reporters, coaches, sports commentators, and salespeople. They give the perception that obtaining a college basketball scholarship is easy if you follow their instructions. What is gravely missing are the voices of parents and players who have succeeded through the process. Most parents are operating in an abyss, while young basketball players seem to worry at ulcer-level proportions about getting their "free ride."

Charlie Scott, *of Laurinburg, SC, was the first African American to ever receive a basketball college scholarship. He received it in 1966 from Dean Smith, who was the head coach at the University of North Carolina.*

In 2020, Jaylen Clark (UCLA Bruins), who received 14 college offers, made a 30-minute YouTube video, *"How to Get DI Basketball Offers Fast!"* It has received over 119,000 views. In the video, Clark provides a candid insider look into the endurance it takes to obtain a basketball scholarship. It is worth viewing by any young basketball player hoping for the same.

Because the basketball college recruiting system is congested, I would have been grateful to hear more stories from student-athletes and parents. Aside from Clark, I could barely find a quote. What I have learned in this grueling process is that the first thing you must find out is whether your son is going to college to play basketball or whether he is playing basketball to go to college.

There is a difference.

Once that is determined, it will route you in the right direction. If it is the latter, a D3 college may be an easier option for parents. Remember that while you and your son hope to be financially free during his college years, most college coaches who distribute scholarships are looking for game-winners, revenue, job stability, and championships!

What is a Basketball Scholarship?

A basketball scholarship is often called a "free ride." On that ride, a college pays for your son's education in exchange for him playing basketball. Critics argue that playing college basketball is far from free and that it is a job with rules and regulations. What do parents believe? What do players think?

As a parent of a son who has been fortunate to receive two D1 scholarships, I have yet to hear a complaint from him. It can be argued that he has been "working" in youth basketball for years, and the earlier ride certainly was not free. Covering college tuition costs undoubtedly helps the parents. Critics aside, today's young basketball players also belong to the first generation who can earn money as amateurs and that also helps parents save money.

"Playing any sport at a high-level is a business. The [college] administration will treat it as a business, and so should you. When you think you've covered all bases, confirm once more."

Cody Sims,
Former player Fordham University

The best scholarships cover everything 100%, such as tuition, books, housing, student fees, meals and limited transportation to and from campus. Team items include uniforms, playing sneakers, and game travel expenses.

However, not all college scholarships cover everything 100% even in D1 colleges. Parents, or the student-athletes themselves, may still have to come out-of-pocket if offered a "partial" scholarship. If you find yourself having to contribute, check with the college's financial aid office to see if there are grants, merit scholarships, and supplemental funds that your son may be eligible for.

A college basketball education can also be paid for by:

- Applying for Federal Student Aid, also known as FAFSA (studentaid.gov).

College Recruitment & Scholarships

- Conducting an online search for grants for athletes, grants for basketball players, grants according to race or ethnicity, etc.
- Alumni scholarships.
- Considering student loan options.

It is also vital to note that basketball scholarships are primarily distributed on a year-to-year basis rather than for the full four years.

Up until 2013, most college players received four-year scholarships. That year, the NCAA overturned that ruling and allowed colleges the option to cover one year, several, or all four. Most have decided to award them on a year-to-year basis, although two conferences require their colleges to give full four-year scholarships.

In 2014, the Big Ten and the Pac-12 conference announced it would guarantee four-year athletic scholarships to its players. Jim Delany, the former Big Ten commissioner, stated, "To make a four-year commitment and give student-athletes the security, it's the right thing to do."[41]

Furthermore, the NCAA has now ruled that college transfer students who receive scholarships are guaranteed financial support at their new school through graduation (or to the end of their basketball eligibility).[42] That is a huge game changer for students who transfer beginning in the 2023-24 academic year. This may also reduce the current competition between high school graduates and transfer students vying for scholarships. If a college coach can offer a high school recruit a one-year scholarship, would they still prioritize a transfer student? This remains to be seen, but high school basketball parents should keep up with the new ruling.

If your son has a year-to-year scholarship, he should find out by the end of the season whether it will be extended for another year. The sooner, the better because it may allow him the opportunity to enter the transfer portal. If his scholarship is not extended for another year, and he disagrees with the decision, he can appeal. The NCAA requires their member institutions to have a student appeal process.

Governing Associations for College Athletics

The following are the governing bodies which set the rules for college athletes, including recruitment. They can also be your go-to source for information and verification.

- The **NCAA** is a nonprofit organization that regulates student athletics in 1,100 schools in the USA (including Puerto Rico) and Canada. The NCAA is the largest collegiate-sanctioning organization. Basketball players make up most sports participants.

  The **NCAA Eligibility Center** (web3.ncaa.org/ecwr3/) establishes your son's academic eligibility and amateurism status. Registration should be done in the 9th grade. He must be registered before he can make any official college visits.

  For potential D1 and D2 athletes, the fee is $100. If your son's high school is not paying the fee, and you cannot afford it, you can request a fee waiver from the NCAA to cover the cost. They also have an informative Twitter account specifically for eligibility @NCAAEC.

  Once registered, your son's account will generate a unique ID which will be used when he completes recruiting questionnaires.

  Mark Emmert, who led the NCAA for 12 years, stepped down in early 2022. In March of 2023, the NCAA will welcome a new president, Charlie Baker, who ended his term as Governor of Massachusetts in 2022.

  The NCAA has also recently created a Division 1 Transformation Committee.[43] Members include college leaders from several conferences who are "building the future of D1 athletics" by "overhauling and modernizing NCAA governance."

  Parents should consider signing up on the NCAA website, or set a Google Alert for the "NCAA Transformation Committee" to receive updates on what college recruitment leaders are referring to as "radical changes"[44] in the near future.

College Recruitment & Scholarships

- ***National Association of Intercollegiate Athletics (NAIA)*** is an association for smaller colleges. The NAIA colleges are also viable options for college basketball scholarships, and more than 30,000 student-athletes register with them each year. Twitter: @NAIA

  The NAIA Eligibility Center (play.mynaia.org) allows parents and athletes to create free profiles. Players may also upload highlight videos for viewing by college coaches.

- **National Junior College Athletic Association (NJCAA)** oversees community colleges, and state and junior college (JUCO) athletics in 525 schools. Twitter: @NJCAA

- **United States Collegiate Athletic Association (USCAA)** is a conference of small colleges, including community and junior colleges (JUCO). Twitter: @USCAA

- **Association of Christian College Athletics (ACCA)** comprises 17 small Christian colleges. Twitter: @ACCA_sport

- **National Christian College Athletic Association (NCCAA)** is an association of Christian and Bible Colleges with 90 members. Twitter: TheNCCAA

College Basketball Conferences

It is not only important to find a college and academic level that fits your son but also a basketball conference that differs based on competition levels. If you follow them early in the process, you will learn the rules a team must follow, their eligibility information, player information, and the team's ranking. This information can aid your son in his college selection. You can also find a list of D1 conferences at espn.com/mens-college-basketball/ conferences.

Kevin Warren, Commissioner of the Big Ten Conference, is the first Black commissioner in any sport in the history of United States sports. He played college basketball at the University of Pennsylvania and Grand Canyon before obtaining his MBA from Arizona State and his J.D. from the Notre Dame School of Law.

Member institutions of governing associations are divided into divisions. The exception is the NAIA, which does not have divisions.

Division I (D1)

Each team has thirteen (13) men's scholarships per year; women have fifteen (15). There are 32 Division 1 conferences.[45] Alaska is the only state without a Division 1 basketball program. Teams likely have fully funded coaching staff; world-class athletic facilities; some travel on their own, or leased, private jets; player support (nutritionists, tutors, and sports psychologists); athlete-only living arrangements; an abundance of playing gear; and access to above-average NIL opportunities.

Players in D1 four-year colleges come from other D1 four-year colleges, post-grad schools, straight from high school, or other countries. These are the colleges that most young basketball players aspire to play at. These are also the teams participating in "The Big Dance," (NCAA March Madness Tournament). The official tournament's name is the NCAA Division 1 Men's (or Women's) Basketball Tournament.

Gloria Nevarez *is the first Latino woman to serve as a D1 conference commissioner (The West Coast Conference) and is one of nine D1 commissioners who are women.*

Top Ten cities that produced the highest number of D1 men's basketball players in 2022:

1. New York City — 101
2. Chicago, IL — 87
3. Houston, TX — 87
4. Philadelphia, PA — 52
5. Atlanta, GA — 51
6. Charlotte, NC — 47
7. Dallas, TX — 42
8. Los Angeles, CA — 41
9. Memphis, TN — 40
10. Baltimore, MD — 40

Source: NCAA.com

COLLEGE RECRUITMENT & SCHOLARSHIPS

Division II (D2)

Each team has ten (10) men's scholarships; women have ten (10). These colleges also have excellent facilities and coaching staff, but their budgets are lower than a D1. D2 colleges mainly offer partial scholarships.

There is an assumption that players who attend D2 schools are less competitive than D1 athletes. Some great professional athletes have attended D2 colleges, including Ben Wallace (Virginia Union), Dennis Rodman (Southern Oklahoma State), Scottie Pippen (Central Arkansas), and Jaylen Morris (Molloy College) who currently plays for the Austin Spurs in the NBA G League.

Division III (D3)

D3 colleges make up the largest number of male basketball players comprising 40% of players. D3 colleges do not generate revenue, and they do not allow any funds to benefit their athletic department. They cannot offer scholarships, but players may receive need-based or merit-based financial aid.

If a player has ambitions of going professional, D3 will likely be his last resort. In addition, players cannot redshirt, and academics take a front seat over sports.

Devean George *(Augsburg University) is the only D3 player ever drafted in the first round of the NBA Draft. He was selected as the 23rd pick for the Los Angeles Lakers in 1999.*

College Division Levels – Finding the Right Fit

There are three terms used by coaches, sports journalists, and student-athletes in college sports to differentiate D1 team levels.

High-Major: Teams are members of the "Power 5" and includes the Big Ten, Atlantic Coast, Big 12, the SEC, the Pacific-12, and the Big East. Members of the media have added the Big East to this conference, and it is often referred to as the "Power 6."

Mid-Major: Teams are members of the following conferences: Missouri Valley, Colonial Athletic, Big Sky, Sun Belt, Ohio Valley, America East, Big East (also considered a High-Major); Conference USA (CUSA), Atlantic 10 (A10), ASUN (formerly the Atlantic Sun Conference), Mid-Atlantic Eastern Conference (MEAC), and the Summit League.

Low-Major: The conferences and schools considered low-major have been through a great deal of debate. Some consider the MEAC (one of the HBCU conferences) as a low-major.

However, the MEAC is proving they can hold their own and are also playing on national stages.

Sonja Stills is the first woman commissioner in MEAC history and the first woman commissioner of a Division 1 HBCU. She has a bachelor's degree from Old Dominion University, a Master of Arts from Hampton University, and she is a graduate of the Sports Management Institute.

Historically Black Colleges and Universities (HBCUs)

Unfortunately, HBCUs are not even presented to most high school basketball players and public discussions are limited. Robert Covington (Tennessee State), who currently plays for the Los Angeles Clippers, is currently the only player in the NBA from a HBCU.

Three former HBCU players were celebrated in the NBA's 75th Anniversary in 2022: Earl "The Pearl" Monroe (Winston Salem); Willis Reed (Grambling), and Sam Jones (North Carolina Central). In the Naismith Basketball Hall of Fame, there are 10 HBCU players, including Charles Oakley (Virginia Union,) one of the league's top rebounders; Ben Wallace (Virginia Union); Anthony Mason

A Great List:

50 Impactful Low Major Coaches in DI Basketball by Jake Stanbrough et al.

College Recruitment & Scholarships

(Tennessee State); and Zelmo Beaty (Prairie A&M), the first HBCU student ever picked in the first round of an NBA draft (1962).

Although there is a long legacy of producing iconic players, HBCU coaches are not a presence at major basketball tournaments or recruitment events. Young players need to see them. Telling parents there is a need for more funding to attend national tournaments or recruiting events is no longer acceptable. HBCUs can create parent booster clubs, or hire fundraisers, just like at other colleges to raise funding.

HBCU leaders and alumni also complain that racial inequities are still factors and a reason they cannot compete against predominantly White institutions (PWIs) for recruits.

When Chad and I showed up for a tour of Morgan State in Baltimore, I wanted him to be impressed. As a potential business major, his first stop was to Morgan's Earl G. Graves School of Business and Management. The building, which cost $80 million to build, is a 140,000 square foot complex complete with a Wall Street trader floor.

Chad said, "This is incredible, but let's go look at the gym."

I learned young athletes are not opposed to playing basketball at a HBCU, they are opposed to the "separate and unequal" facilities.

Yet, Chad soon learned there were upscale basketball perks as a student-athlete at Morgan, including world-class academics, playing basketball on a national stage, and coincidentally, working out in the same fitness center, with the college's president at the crack of dawn. His coaches, professors, and advisors all pushed him to succeed academically which was tremendously important to me. His choice to leave after two years came down to two things: the athletic director and several coaches close to Chad left for jobs elsewhere, and he was ready to play in a "higher" conference.

Although I wanted him to stay at Morgan, and possibly be an example for other young players coming after him, I had to support his college decision—as long as he stayed on the path to obtain his bachelor's degree. One thing is for sure, it was an appreciated and viable start to his college academic life and basketball career.

THE PARENT'S SECTION: OUTSIDE THE LOCKER ROOM

If an HBCU is a college interest, your son may need to reach out to coaches himself. Unfortunately, I have also seen quite a few videos on social media from top players who stated they wanted to go to an HBCU, but their requests went unanswered. Do not give up, keep trying.

HBCUs participate in the following conferences:

Mid-Eastern Athletic Conference (MEAC), Southwest Athletic Conference (SWAC), Southern Intercollegiate Conference (SIAC), the Gulf Coast Athletic Conference (GCAC) and the Central Intercollegiate Athletic Association (CIAA). The CIAA Conference is the nation's oldest Black athletic conference and is led by Jacqie McWilliams, who was the first woman commissioner of an HBCU conference. Each year, the CIAA hosts a large and phenomenal basketball tournament.

In 2022, the event was held at the former Royal Farms Arena (now the CFG Bank Arena) in Baltimore. Attendance was estimated at 36,000 over a five-day period.

HBCU players do not lack talent as some believe. In 2020, when Morgan State beat Iona and Delaware State, those opposing teams were shocked. The Norfolk State Spartans, formerly a D2 college in the CIAA Conference, have made it to March Madness for two years in a row (2020 and 2021).

Hopefully, the tide is slowly changing with the recent HBCU investments from others:

- The NBA has announced an ongoing commitment to "new programs designed to create greater opportunity for students and alumni, encourage economic advancement, and further celebrate their rich traditions."[46]

- The 2022 NBA All-Star game featured the first-ever NBA HBCU Classic with Morgan State vs. Howard presented by AT&T in Cleveland. Chad was the starting center for the Morgan State Bears. Keke Palmer sang the national anthem, and countless celebrities were in attendance, including Spike Lee and the Reverend Jesse Jackson. It was a phenomenal experience for all the players who were treated like VIPs. Players spent time with several NBA players, including Trae Young (Atlanta Hawks), Stephen Curry (Golden State

COLLEGE RECRUITMENT & SCHOLARSHIPS

Warriors), Cole Anthony (Orlando Magic), Andrew Wiggins (Golden State Warriors), and Chris Paul (Phoenix Suns). Both teams had an opportunity to film a Google Pixel 6 commercial with celebrity photographer Shaniqwa Jarvis. It has garnered over 1.3 million YouTube views.

- In November of 2021, Chris Paul, a graduate of the HBCU Winston-Salem State, and who sits on President Joe Biden's Board of Advisors for HBCUs, hosted the inaugural Boost Mobile Chris Paul HBCU Challenge. Four teams had the opportunity to play at the Footprint Center in Phoenix (Morgan State, Norfolk State, Grambling, and Hampton).

- In April of 2022, the inaugural HBCU All-Star game, founded by Travis L. Williams, occurred during the NCAA Final Four weekend in New Orleans. The game featured the best seniors in HBCU basketball. The next game is set to take place in April of 2023 in Houston and will be sponsored by CBS Sports.

- Media mogul, Byron Allen, has created the free-streaming digital platform HBCU GO which provides coverage of 107 HBCUs, including the SWAC and CIAA conferences on CBS-owned-and-operated stations in several cities. Allen stated,

> *"We are proud to amplify these amazing athletes and HBCUs, while at the same time helping to finance the education of these young adults. Now sports fans across the country will have access to best-in-class games from America's HBCUs."*[47]

HBCUs should not be overlooked as a viable educational and basketball option by any high school basketball player and parent, regardless of race.

One of my favorite HBCU players, besides Will Thomas at Morgan State, is one of Chad's former roommates, Ty Horner. Ty is a Caucasian, 6'10" senior from Oregon who transferred to Morgan State from the North Dakota College of Science where he was an All-League First Team selection. Although Ty's career goal is to become a venture capitalist, he plays his center position well for the Bears and appears to be doing well at Morgan.

Junior College (JUCOs)

When coaches tell a player they should "go JUCO" the player may automatically feel that he is not good enough to play at a four-year college.

Many factors go into playing college basketball, including grades, and overall GPA, etc. Parents and players should treat junior colleges like a general student who may have to start there before transferring to a four-year college.

Before high school players consider a D2 college, youth coaches encourage them to go this route. Although it would appear to make more sense to consider a D2 four-year college over a JUCO, at least academically, in the basketball world, it is different. JUCO players have a recruitment advantage over D2 and high school recruits.

In 2018, 14.8% of all JUCO basketball players transferred to a four-year NCAA D1 college program compared to less than 2% of high-school basketball players who went on to play D1 basketball.[48]

JUCOs also have some great and modern facilities for their basketball teams, as well great coaches. Some also offer housing on campus.

JUCOs have produced the following successful players:

- Jimmy Butler (Miami Heat) played for Tyler Junior College.
- Jae Crowder (Phoenix Suns) played at South Georgia Technical College and Howard College.
- Steve Francis (a former player with the Houston Rockets, Orlando Magic, and the New York Knicks) went to Allegany Community
- Dennis Rodman played at North Central Texas before heading to Southeastern Oklahoma State.
- Avery Johnson, the former head coach of the Brooklyn Nets and the Alabama Crimson Tide, also started at New Mexico Junior College.

The JUCO route is a feasible option for players who:

College Recruitment & Scholarships

- Have not received any scholarship offers.
- Did not qualify for full NCAA eligibility.
- Were not admitted to a four-year college due to grades or a GPA.
- Did not receive enough financial assistance to attend a four-year college.
- Believes he will not play during his first, or second year at a four-year college.
- Has the need to further develop his basketball skills.

Basketball Ratings and Rankings

Most scouting services, such as ESPN and Rivals, classify recruits by "stars." Five stars are the highest, with two stars as the lowest. No major recruiting service issues ratings below two stars.

As a parent, you should know that national ratings and rankings are extremely important to high school players. They may be right behind in getting their first offer. It may provide added confidence for the Top 100 players, but for the 540,700 others, it can mean frustration and pure torture.

Chad played basketball non-stop for four years of high school, including every summer on great AAU teams. He did well during his post-graduate year, had media coverage, and was ranked fairly decently regionally and statewide. He was, as they say, in the basketball world, "getting looks." Yet, he was rated a two-star all through high school when he sometimes competed, and defended exceptionally well, against four- and five-star players who could barely score on him.

Chad persistently looked for his national rating and ranking so much that I reached out to every service that compiles them to learn how determinations were made.

No one responded.

Chad pressed on, believing one day they would come.

To this day, Chad is not listed on the Rivals site, although they hail themselves as "The country's No. 1 authority on college football and basketball recruiting."

I will never forget a popular AAU coach in New York City who, after a tryout and looking up Chad's "star" rating on his phone, shared that Chad "would be lucky to get a D2 college offer with his two stars."

Yet, he failed to tell us how to accomplish it. When I asked, "How does he do that?" He seemed surprised but had no answer.

That conversation put me on track to search and learn about college division levels, as well as seek information from several of my cousins who played at D2 colleges. It is then that I learned that the coach may have been trying to insult Chad. One of my cousins said, "Chad is 6'10" and can play, he is definitely going D1."

Thankfully, college coaches saw him outside of a star and rating system. I had to remind Chad that his goal for playing basketball was not to be rated, or ranked. Nor was he playing for the opinions of anyone who did not believe in his talent, or his potential to get better on the court. We also later found out stars and rankings mean little to college coaches in the recruiting process.

Social Media

Twitter's *direct messages are the go-to source for college coaches, recruiters and agents.*

Instagram (IG) *is another source for outreach efforts. It is also where many student-athletes and college teams share their photos.*

Facebook (FB) *is not a huge place for basketball recruitment, perhaps because players who are a part of Generation Z and Millennials, believe FB is for older people and families. However, the FB group, "Basketball Market for Players and Coaches" is worth a look.*

Daymond Sayles, in the *Bleacher Report* notes:

"When it comes to ratings, however, most college coaches will downplay a recruit's stars—whether he's a 5-star athlete or a 2-star athlete. In the eyes of college coaches, it's not what a player is doing now that's most important; it's the potential he must excel at the next level."[49]

College Recruitment & Scholarships

Ja Morant (Memphis Grizzlies) was also rated two stars in high school and had zero offers. Yet, Morant ended up, after playing two years at Murray State, a first-round, number two NBA draft pick by the Memphis Grizzlies in 2021. Morant is currently considered one of the top talents in the NBA under 25 years old.

Stephen Curry (Golden State Warriors) was rated three stars and barely had any offers out of high school. He ended up at what is considered, for argument's sake, a mid-major college (Davidson). Today, he is hailed as the best three-point shooter to ever play basketball.

For those who are rated and ranked, great. If your son is not, tell him not to worry. Keep going!

Preparing for Recruitment

In his Masterclass, Stephen Curry shared: "My senior year of high school I wasn't getting recruited as heavily as I thought I was supposed to." Curry added, "The waiting process of trying to get recruited was really stressful. It really nagged at me pretty much every day."[50]

The prolific words from the son of a former NBA player.

Growing up, Curry likely had all the resources of private trainers, great facilities, and the expertise from his father, yet he worried just like many other young players. However, it made me realize there is nothing that will replace the hard work a young basketball player must put in and the continuous support they may need from their parents to get through stressful times.

Since there are thousands of players each year, and limited scholarships, coaches and their staff may not spend too much time on one. If a coach, or a member of a coaching staff, reaches out to you or your son, consider yourself lucky. It means they probably see something they can work with in the future.

Coaches seek players with potential and who will fit into their coaching style. They will find out a player's basketball IQ, their ability to defend the ball, and whether they are great scorers, rebounders, etc.

They want to know a player will help them win, not play selfishly, as if they are giving personal solos. If your son has a temper problem, cannot take instruction, has ever had public conflicts (including on the court), or uses drugs, he may get passed over. Your son should always be ready to explain why they believe they would be an asset to a team and a college. If needed, parents can help practice the answers, including many subjects covered in this book that others will not likely discuss (e.g., your son's interest in their conference).

During recruitment, your son should always respond to any inquiry, even if they are not interested in that college. He can send a quick note or return the call and say, "Thank you for reaching out, can I keep in touch and get back to you?" Coaches change positions all the time, and he may try and recruit your son later. Worst case scenario, that coach remembers that your son ignored him and will not reach out again. Coaches may converse with other recruiters and bring up your son's name. You do not ever want one of them to say, "We reached out to him and never heard back, but I see he posts regularly on social media." Others may believe your son will do the same to them. If your son is not interested but still has no signed commitments, he should leave his recruitment open and be courteous.

The college recruitment process requires a great deal of information sharing. If there are coaches who can pick up the phone, or share a tweet on your son's behalf, ask them to please do so.

Your son should have the following readily available:

- **His current height, weight, and the position he plays** (be specific, e.g., small forward, shooting guard, etc.).

    Refrain from lying about your son's height. This occurs regularly in grassroots basketball, but it will not work in college. A player's weight can be worked on, but coaches say, "We cannot teach height."

    Former NBA player Spud Webb, the president of basketball operations for the Texas Legends G League team, played impressive basketball at 5'6" and even won an NBA slam dunk contest. Even if your son is short, it may not be a hindrance. Honesty is still the best policy.

- **Student transcript.** Coaches will accept unofficial transcripts, but you can also order official transcripts from Parchment.com.
- **Basketball film highlight video(s):** Covered in Chapter VII.
- **Current coach's name and phone number.** Coaches will definitely make reference checks. They will call to find out if your son is coachable, ask about his grades, demeanor, and his family. One coach told us they even contacted one of Chad's former teammates.
- **A list of any offers.** Verbalcommits.com posts all offers, and they do it in record time. They also appear to be 100% accurate. Some players

  and parents have a bad habit of bragging about non-existent or perceived offers. Verbal Commits is the place others confirm accuracy. You should also make it a habit to check there if your son has received any offers that you may not be aware of. It is alleged that fake offers may appear and is a strategy used by coaches and handlers. If that is the case, you should immediately contact your son's coach and the offeror.

- **Student Accolades.** If your son has received any awards, special recognitions, news stories, or has done volunteer service, be sure to share them.
- **Social media handle and current phone number.** Coaches will contact potential recruits via social media, texts, and the phone (make sure your son checks his voicemail).

  Your son should have a social media name that is easy to find and is identifiable to him. His real name is likely best. Ask your son to add your email to his social media notifications. This way, you can remind him, if necessary, to respond to a coach and keep up with any interest. Tons of coaches contacted Chad this way, and there were so many he would forget to answer them, did not check regularly, or did not have the time to respond. All communications should contain complete sentences, and try to avoid using slang and emojis.

- **Good Manners.** When your son speaks with coaches, he should refer to them as "Coach," "Mr.", or "Ms." They should also make good use of the words "please" and "thank you." Parents should also plan to speak with many coaches. When Chad was in high school, I had to make a folder in my phone contacts just for coaches. The best way I found to keep up with them was to save them immediately after connecting.

Where Do Coaches Find Players?

There is a common saying in basketball circles, "If you're good enough, coaches will find you."

That could be true, if your son is a phenomenal high school player and a stand-out among his counterparts, or has a famous last name. It is also true for players who are considered in the Top 100 in the country.

Top 100 out of 540,800 male high school basketball players.

Finding talented players is not hard and coaching staff travel year-round to search for them. The challenge is finding players who truly want to be great and who will work in college to help their team win.

Networking helps tremendously. Potential recruits are recommended by other coaches, their athletic directors, high school coaches, trainers, and current players on the team recruiting them. Coaches also attend games, tournaments, and even mail postcards/flyers inviting players to camps and showcases. Players also end up on a coach's radar because the player reached out to them on their own. This also shows a player is serious about their recruitment. Emails helped Chad get inquiries from several coaches and invitations to attend college basketball camps at Columbia and Princeton, where Howard's coach also saw him play.

The NBA and USA Basketball have reached an agreement that now allows front-office staff to look for players at 16 and under national camps and tournaments. You can read more about it in the article by Jonathan Givony entitled, *NBA Teams Allowed To Scout High School Players At Key Events.*

The recruitment process is hit or miss for players, coaches and parents. The process needs an overhaul and a formal process. A process that evaluates high school and post-grad recruits like the professional leagues. For example, the NBA Combine is a highly organized event where prospects showcase their talent for NBA teams.

Prospects are interviewed and take personality tests. They perform athletic tests, run drills, and have medical tests where even their body fat percentage is determined. The evaluation is to determine their potential to play professionally. A similar investment in youth basketball would undoubtedly help all involved.

Here are the possible benefits:

- Players will know what level they are on, who has a serious interest, and why.
- Coaches would have empirical data and reliable information on recruits, which would show their productivity and potential before they made them an offer.
- The number of players in the transfer portal would likely decrease.
- Parents would know their role, save money and time while helping their son make a huge life decision.

When to Engage with Coaches

The NCAA has rules for when D1 and D2 student-athletes, parents, and coaches can engage with one another. There are no rules for D3, or NAIA recruits, who may communicate at any time.

The NCAA provides an annual recruitment calendar on its website. There are heavy sanctions if anyone is found to be in violation of the contact rules, including your son losing his eligibility. The recruitment calendar is divided into the following periods:

- ***Contact (or Live) Period:*** When a coach can communicate with a recruit. Contacts can be made via phone, email, text, social media, in-person during a home visit, on campus, or at a game. This is the period when coaches are the most active in their recruitment.
- ***Dead Period:*** There is no in-person, face-to-face contact. Coaches can still reach out via phone, email, text, or social media.
- ***Quiet Period:*** This period is set up to give recruits a break from recruiting. A coach may not contact a recruit except on a college campus. Coaches may not visit their school or their home.
- ***Evaluation Period:*** Coaches can watch players in a game at school or a tournament, but cannot communicate with them outside of a

coach's college campus. Coaches can still reach out via phone, email, text, or social media from their campus.

Reaching Out to Coaches

You may find it a challenge reaching a head coach via email because their emails are not always listed on the team's website. You can search for them in the overall college's staff directory, on Twitter or LinkedIn. As an alternative, you can email the recruiting director or assistant coaches, who also screen potential recruits.

Sample Email to Coaches and Recruiters:

Subject: Name, Height, Weight, Position, Current School

Dear Coach (Last Name of Coach or Staff Member),

My name is _____. I am __ years old. I am in the (grade) at (name of school) in (city, state).

I am writing to ask that you keep me on your radar as a potential (year) recruit. I am told I have the right ingredients that a coach would likely appreciate and much to offer. My highlight video is located here (link to online videos).

- (List GPA and any academic awards).
- Excellent size – (height, weight, and if known: wingspan, vertical jump)
- Good grassroots experience (name of team and location)

(If applicable, add information about his current team that stands out).

I am very coachable and work hard. My goal this year is to improve my (insert information). I would like to major in X at your school.

My current coach is (name of coach), and he/she can be reached at (phone).

Thank you for your time.

I look forward to hearing from you, or a representative.

Sincerely,

Name

Phone Number | Email | Social Media Handle (Twitter and Instagram)

College Recruitment & Scholarships

Basketball Resume

Eurobasket.com has an excellent video on creating a professional basketball resume that young players may find useful. You can find it at europrobasket.com and search "How to make a basketball resume."

Verbal Commitment (An Offer)

A verbal commitment is a way to let a recruit know they are being recruited by a coach and a college.

A recruit may receive several offers, which may even be made public. However, it is crucial to remember that there is no guarantee that the recruit will ever hear from those colleges again. Nor is a college obliged to tell your son why they may no longer be interested.

Kim English, the head basketball coach at George Mason, says,

> *"Offers really used to mean something to coaches. They really used to mean it was bound--it was binding, it was like my word is my bond."*[51]

Although meaningful, recruits should never let a verbal commitment end their recruitment. Recruits like to post verbal commitments, as well as offers, on their social media. It is their attempt to show gratitude, and most of them always include the line: "Blessed to receive an offer from (college name)."

English, who was drafted by the Detroit Pistons in 2012, has another perspective,

> *"The advent of social media and the offer game [has] become disingenuous, [players] want to post that I'm blessed. You're not blessed, you're bragging. It kind of saturated the strength or the value of offers."*

Student-athletes are not the only ones who post. College recruiters also post when a recruit may be visiting for all the world to see. A major factor to remember is that nothing is guaranteed until a National Letter of Intent (NLI), or its equivalent, is signed. Up until signing, scholarship offers and commitments can be dropped by either side, for any reason.

In addition, your son can have his whole college basketball future planned out with the coaching staff and at any time, including the final hour, the college admissions office can deny his admittance. It happened to Chad, and no one prepared us for it. It was a devastating blow weeks before the start of his freshman college year.

Chad received a verbal commitment to a college and, we assumed the compliance office reviewed and signed off on his transcript and eligibility. Coaches and Chad worked on logistics, which also included his move-in date. Chad was ecstatic to be going to a team where a few of his classmates were also attending. The admissions director denied his admission for reasons I will not claim to understand. He suggested Chad attend another college for one semester and then apply as a transfer student.

When I heard that, I thought, "Sir, that is not how student-athletes do this." It was already late August, and time was waning. The coaches were upset and shared that this had "never happened" in their careers. They relayed, "Once the coach makes an offer, the school accepts the student."

Chad was lucky that he had other offers, but the scholarships were already filled because we believed he was locked in at this college. Also, what happens to the student-athlete that may only have one offer?

The year Chad was supposed to enroll, the college was penalized by the NCAA due to misappropriations to basketball and tennis players. They were placed on a two-year probation and fined. A college representative called it a "misunderstanding." The head coach and assistant coach who recruited Chad left.

Years later, while watching one of Chad's games, I recognized the former head coach who was a commentator. I doubt he even remembered Chad, or wondered whatever happened to him.

During the game, he highlighted Chad and shared great comments about him, but mom never forgot the stress placed upon our family. The struggle it took to get Chad committed to another college just days (which seemed like minutes) before the fall semester was starting. Our family will forever be grateful to Morgan State University, their Bears, Coach Kevin Broadus and Coach Julius Allen.

The moral of the story is **never to trust any verbal conversations,** no matter how good they sound.

National Letter of Intent (also known as a "NIL") is a binding contract committing a student-athlete to an NCAA college via a scholarship offer. You can do an internet search for "sample basketball letter of intent" and search under images to find examples.

Although they are not mandatory to sign, the NIL is used by approximately 650 NCAA D1 and D2 colleges. The NAIA and NJCAA (JUCO) colleges have their own versions of a NIL that differ from the NCAA version. For D3 colleges, in lieu of a NIL, players sign a "Celebratory Signing Form."

Once a NIL or another agreement is signed, the recruiting process ends, and other colleges are prohibited from recruiting that player. If your son signs a NIL and the coach who offered the scholarship leaves the program, unlike a verbal commitment, your son's contract with the school remains. If he changes his mind, he can apply for an NCAA waiver to request permission to play immediately at another college. He can provide them with extenuating circumstances as to why he cannot fulfill his obligation at the current college. An example is the coach who recruited him has departed. If he is denied, he will need to sit out for one season if he transfers.

The NCAA has an extremely fair and equitable process for waivers. They are also excellent at providing information to parents and student-athletes upon request, so do not hesitate to contact them with questions or concerns. A college compliance's office also has in-depth knowledge of the waiver process and the rules for student-athletes.

National Signing Day is a big celebration day for high school seniors. Early signing occurs for one week in November. Regular signing is for one month from April to May. Some high schools set up a photo opportunity with a student-athlete and their family members. The media may be also in attendance. Players will wear an item representing their new school and are staged to sign their NIL.

Visits During the Evaluation Process

Home Visits

College coaches may conduct a home visit to their top recruits during the recruiting process. A home visit is huge sign they are serious about his recruitment and an official college visit may soon be on the horizon. Only the parents and the recruit should participate in the home. You should also ensure there are no distractions. Coaches may bring a marketing deck with information on their program's record and college. Be hospitable. Offer your guest something to drink and perhaps a light snack, as the coach may have traveled hours to visit with you and your son.

Do not worry about a tour of the house or your son's room. You will probably not be asked to show it. If your son has special trophies or accolades, you can have them on display.

You should prepare for a candid conversation about college basketball overall and your son's possible future with the team. During the visit, the coach may be laid back, but he is watching the interaction between you and your son. Is he respectful to you? Is he courteous? Who wants basketball success more? Who controls the narrative? He needs to know he is making the correct decision by adding your son to his roster and the college "family." Let your son do most of the talking, even if you have questions.

> *"Recruits often attempt to tell a coach why they like the program or school. But often don't elaborate as to why they would like to play for a specific coach.*
> *Do this!— It will go a long way."*
> Coach William Payne

Unofficial and Official College Visits

Visiting a prospective college campus is critical to the recruiting process. There are two types of visits: unofficial and official.

College Recruitment & Scholarships

An **official visit** is when the college invites a student-athlete to campus and covers all the expenses. Recruits may visit with or without their parents. Recruits are also allowed to receive complimentary tickets to any home games during their visit. Each official visit can last up to 48 hours. Recruits are allowed five official visits at the D1 and D2 levels. Official visits are a fast and intense experience.

The coaches, and their staff, are pros at it. We received a written itinerary and agenda that reminded me of a run of show for an event production. The marketing collateral featured PowerPoint slides and video highlights of Chad. They shared background information they had on Chad from references. They mentioned accolades about him that even I had forgotten about. Every minute was covered—from the moment we walked out of our front door to our arrival on campus; to when we left for our hotel or to go home. I lost track of time on several occasions.

It was an extremely hospitable affair. There were excellent group meals, campus tours, and comfortable accommodations. They also had a uniform ready for Chad to do a photoshoot, in which I was invited to participate. If all goes well, at the end of the visit, that coach will expect a commitment before your son departs.

An **unofficial visit** is anytime a recruit (with or without their parents) visits a college, but the expenses are not paid by the college. The college may only provide complimentary tickets to a home game. A recruit has an unlimited number of unofficial visits, and they can begin at any time. A good idea would be for your son to request unofficial visits to schools he would like to attend during their basketball season while in high school. It shows a large interest from a recruit.

Preparing for Your Official Visit: It is a Two-Way Street

- Parents, make sure your son brings his A game!
- Make sure he has a haircut, or his hair and grooming is presentable as if he were going on a job interview (minus the dress clothes).
- Tell your son to be himself! Let his personality and his character shine.

The Parent's Section: Outside The Locker Room

- Your son should be ready to play basketball; be sure to bring playing clothes, on the court sneakers, and a small towel.
- Pack light with casual clothing and comfortable shoes, as you may be walking a lot around campus. Ask if you need to bring any formal dress attire.
- Bring your laptop if you need it to work, your phone charger, and a notepad.
- Do not schedule any other appointments during your visit as you will be preoccupied.
- If you have questions about the college overall, it is best to visit on the weekdays, so you have time to speak with school administrators.
- Do not worry about meal expenses, as they will be covered by the college.
- Bring a copy of your son's transcript.

Official visits are opportunities for recruits to see the campus and facilities, as well as meet and attend practice with the basketball team. Although much information was shared with us, here are a few questions I had during Chad's home and college visits.

- What do you like most about my son's skillset?
- What accommodations are made when a player travels and may miss class or have an assignment due?
- Are you planning on staying as the head coach for the next few years?
- What is the graduation rate for your players?
- How does the team travel to away games?
- How do you see Chad benefitting your team?
- Is it possible to tour where he will live on or off campus?
- What is the neighborhood like around campus?
- How does the community support the team?

College Recruitment & Scholarships

- Is there a booster club?
- Where do you see Chad in two years?
- Is there a nutritionist on staff?
- What type of academic support is provided to players?

While on the visit, someone should definitely inquire who else is being recruited for the same position as your son. You can ask about the number of seniors on the team in your son's position which may give you an idea of when the spot will open for him to play. You can look for their recruiting board (usually in the head coach's office) to see what positions are open, the names of other recruits, etc. You can also find other recruits offered on verbalcommits.com.

If your son is a college transfer student, you may also want to ask how many credits are transferable. This is profoundly important. You do not want to put your son in a position to either repeat classes they have already taken or delay his potential graduation date. You can ask whether there is an appeal process if credits are not transferable. One college shared that they had one.

Although the official visits for Chad went well, there was also a downside. We learned that when booked to visit, even then, there is no guarantee.

Chad was recruited by another college. Their process began with two weeks of non-stop phone calls and texts. They also conducted a video meeting with Chad, me, and their entire coaching staff. They proclaimed to be among the best coaching staff and role models who cared for their players, on and off the court. They told Chad how great he was and propped him up as a player. They shared that they were eager to meet him in person. Afterwards, an official visit was scheduled to take place the following weekend.

The contact with us increased. Almost daily, I felt I had to reassure them that Chad would be attending. They clearly wanted Chad to select them over his other offers.

Sadly, we found out that everything that glitters is not gold.

The Parent's Section: Outside The Locker Room

We were scheduled to leave on a Friday morning at 8 am.

The day prior to leaving, we received several calls and texts to "check in." I was even asked if I wanted anything "special" from the city we were visiting. Then they dropped a nuclear explosion.

At 10 pm the night before our departure, with our bags packed and alarms set, the assistant coach and the trip's organizer called Chad with the news. Their team had accepted the commitment from another recruit for his position. And just like that, our visit was canceled. Chad's recruitment was off the table. I heard the familiar voice on the other line state, "I'm so sorry about this. This is just the way of this business, but we wish you all the best in your career. I will be giving your mom a call."

He never did.

Parents, it does not matter that a college may have made it public that your son intends to visit their campus, thereby possibly pushing away another college that may have been interested. It does not matter that you may have to take time off from your job for the visit.

Although it was not the first lesson on basketball adversity my son had ever faced, it was the largest. At that point, my son was not a 6'10" young man. I saw him as the toddler he once was asking mommy to pick him up. I knew he was an adult, and I decided I could not give him any pity. He had to learn how to conquer setbacks on his own. Even now, as I write this and think back to that day, my eyes are watering. Chad kept his pride, shrugged it off, and said, "Ma, that's just how this goes."

What I learned is that although Chad's rejection was another opportunity for a young man to play D1 basketball, I knew my son was hurt. Once again, I prayed that God would put him in the right place at the right time. I questioned whether I should try and convince him to call back his coach at Morgan to return. Chad had done well there. Ultimately, I decided he had to handle this on his own.

That Friday, it poured rain.

Chad slept all day.

College Recruitment & Scholarships

Selecting a College

After years of watching my son and others in my family play basketball, I have learned that a player needs to select a coach over a team.

I think back to all the times anyone in my family ever soared playing basketball. It was not the team they were on, or the school, it was the coach that brought out the best in them. The coach who believed in them.

I quit basketball in the 8th grade because my coach cursed at me after I fell during a championship game. I was on the floor with a twisted ankle in pain, and he never stopped yelling. He could have cared less that I had to limp home.

Players need coaches who believe in them and who care about them. Coaches with integrity and empathy. A coach who says upfront what they can and cannot do.

For example, not all coaches, or trainers, are the best with big men who play the center position. You will need to connect your son with a coach who can teach your son's position.

Although parents have to be methodical and find college options that are realistically the best all-around fit for your son, look for a coach that can *and* wants to coach your son.

Many athletes want to attend colleges with high name recognition, such as those referred to as the Blue Bloods (Duke, University of North Carolina, Kansas, Kentucky, etc.). They have large athletic budgets, great facilities, skillful players, and great coaches. Their players are

Blue Blood Origins
January 3, 1927
The Time Union in Brooklyn featured a sub-headline, "Centrals Made Up of Basketball Blue Bloods." The term referred to basketball teams in 1946 when Dick Dunkel had a men's basketball rating system in The Charlotte News.
Source: Andy Wittry, NCAA.com

treated like rock stars. The promotion for them is high level. They travel in private jets. Their facilities are equipped like professional arenas. Parents and handlers may be full of pride and boosted egos. Their coach may be famous, and the fan base is huge. Chad says no player will turn down an opportunity to play in the Power 5 (or Power 6) conference. That is understandable however, there is a saying,

> **"It may be better to be a gigantic fish in a small pond, than a regular fish in a large pond."**

Why would a player choose to become a redshirt freshman at a high major college when they could possibly be a starting freshman at another? In particular, if the other college has a similar academic record.

There are countless college players no longer playing basketball because they made the mistake of selecting a college for the name, the brand, or its social standing.

As a result, many players cannot transition from high school stardom to college and beyond. These players get to college and realize that most freshmen start at ground zero. They find out that college playing time is earned. Most will need to learn from veteran players, as well as their new coach's system. There is also nothing that says "I am done" on this team more than a player averaging 1-2 minutes or no minutes per season. That part is not shared with recruits. It is heartbreaking to learn of players who go through the psychological 360 degrees.

Each day, a serious player is working and improving to get to the next level. The worst thing that could happen, outside of an injury, is your son sitting on a bench and not being able to play competitively in college. It is an entirely different level from youth basketball.

This places them at a disadvantage on the court, and psychologically off the court. Time can go fast, and before you know it, they have low stats, and their college eligibility is over.

What can you do as a parent to help a player before it gets to that?

Ask college coaches, who have never coached your son to evaluate him and get their perspectives on a good college fit. Many times, I reached out to random coaches, shared my son's film, and asked their opinion of "his basketball level." I also read sports analysts' comments and listened intently to game commentators when he played.

Chad always had the largest (and best) sense of where he could make an impact and help a team. He is also the one who taught me about the differences in college conferences. I have heard him and other players say they picked their college because it felt like "home" or a "family." Without a doubt, the head coach created that environment.

There is also a popular saying in basketball that a player should,

> **"Go where you are wanted, not tolerated."**

As a parent, you should want your son to be comfortable at college, just like any other college student. Thankfully, it has worked out for Chad. The majority of his coaches have been good people, and although they have integrity and are impactful, they are about business every step of the way. They also know how to create a culture of care for their players. With due diligence and always having a backup plan, positive results can be achieved.

College is a major decision, and you must always treat it as such.

Holding Out for Better Offers

One of basketball's most revered coaches said it best,

> *"The bigger your head, the easier to fill your shoes."*
> —Phil Jackson

Most high school basketball players will not get an opportunity to play college basketball on any level, in any division. Far too many parents and players make the mistake of holding out for extra offers or D1 only offers.

The reality is that the odds of a high school basketball player making a D1 basketball roster is 105:1. An even smaller number will receive a scholarship. Making it on any college basketball roster is 18:1.

The Parent's Section: Outside The Locker Room

> *"Yeah, I see too many kids get so discouraged because they're expecting to make this quantum leap. And when that quantum leap doesn't come, it feels like it will never come right. But that's not how it works. It's step by step. One foot in front of the other. Day by day get better every single day. And then when you look back, then you look down at the mountain you just scaled. But you can't jump from the bottom of [Mount] Everest to get to the top of Everest like that. Superman is only in comics."*
> *Kobe Bryant*

If a college has shown your son commitment, great hospitality and has recruited him professionally, advise him to accept their offer, especially if it is a D1 and/or covers him 100%. Why take a gamble?

Do not let fancy social media mixtapes give the perception that your son will definitely receive a scholarship or that he can take his time. It may not get any better, no matter how great his grades are or how good he plays. If your son would like to delay a commitment, he should find out when is the latest he can accept the offer from the head coach.

People may also try and persuade your son that he still has time. The more he delays, a coach may start to have doubts, or another recruit may accept. If your son decides to circle back, it may be too late.

I have watched players, with verbal offers, or no offers, trying to find a college at the end of the AAU season (end of July). You will also find coaches on Twitter still recruiting as well.

By the end of May, in their senior or post-graduate year, your son should have already accepted a scholarship if he had viable options. College basketball players arrive on campus at the beginning of June, not in late August, like most students.

A college education is a valuable accolade. For me, it is as American as apple pie and helps alleviate poverty. I have helped thousands of young people get not only their undergraduate degrees but doctorates, medical and law degrees. I have helped them find the financial resources to do so, which can be challenging. Obtaining a scholarship, especially a

College Recruitment & Scholarships

full scholarship, is a blessing, no matter the college or conference.

There are over a thousand players in the college transfer portal, with more added each year. Coaches go there first. As a result, the transfer portal has also made it more competitive for high school players to get recruited. As noted earlier, a coach is more likely to seek a player who already has college experience.

A select group of players now also have an extra year of eligibility due to COVID because their seasons were canceled or cut short. That extra year seems extremely appealing to coaches and gave another advantage over high school graduates.

Holding out is not the best strategy.

No Scholarship Offer? It is Not Over.

If your son did not obtain a scholarship out of high school or through the transfer portal, they can still go on and be successful in basketball. Here are other options to get into college and play basketball. One, is to consider your son doing a post-graduate year at a prep school, or a basketball academy as noted in Chapter III. The following are options for college:

Walk-On

It is possible that your son can walk onto a team by trying out for it. Coaches may also ask student-athletes to walk on if they see value in them, but they do not have any scholarship money left. They will usually promise a scholarship in year two. If this is an option, ask for honesty from the coach and find out the likelihood your son will play and when.

Red Shirt Freshman

A redshirt freshman is a student-athlete who has been awarded a scholarship but cannot play for one year. Players can participate in all team activities, such as practice, training, and travel with the team.

Reasons for being redshirted include a coach wanting a year to physically prepare an athlete for college competition.

A "medical redshirt" is used for an injured player.

The Parent's Section: Outside The Locker Room

A student-athlete can also be an "academic redshirt" because they have not met all their academic eligibility requirements.

It should be noted that a sophomore and junior redshirt is the term currently given to student-athletes who have an extra COVID year, and it differs from a redshirt freshman. For example, although Chad is an academic junior (for classes and his graduation class), he is listed as a redshirt sophomore for basketball. The extra COVID year means college players have six years of eligibility instead of the traditional five years.

Apply to College as a General Student

I believe many parents and players get so caught up in basketball as the only option to college. I would like to mention most students enter college through an application process.

As a backup plan and to cover all bases, Chad applied and was accepted to several great colleges as a general student. My rationale for was that it was time for Chad to go to college whether he had a basketball scholarship or not. Although a long shot, I believed that once a basketball coach saw my 6'10" son, he would give him a chance to tryout and he would make the team.

Recruiting and Scouting Services

Another source of help are recruiting and scouting services.

These privately-owned companies advertise that they connect student-athletes with college coaches and will aid in recruitment. *USA Today High School Sports* refers to them as "A real gamble."[52] They also report that their services can have one-time fees from $100 to $3,000.

Parents should use their discernment to decide if recruiting services are worth an investment. Some may advertise that they provide "NCAA approved" services, but that does not mean they are endorsed, or recommended, by the NCAA. The NCAA provides "approval," for D1 coaches to "access" information in their recruiting services portal.

For Chad, they offered great access to D2 and D3 basketball coaches and gave us good advice on the process. Their websites also contain information parents may find useful.

Final Thoughts on Recruitment & Securing a College Scholarship

There are many doors to success and more than one way to obtain a basketball college scholarship. More options are opening for high school players to skip college altogether, and you can read about the alternatives in Chapter IX.

Whatever road you find your son on, never stop believing he can succeed, and all the best to him!

CHAPTER VI

Health & Wellness

"We often look at athletes as MACHINES and we do not look at them as HUMANS."

— **Darius Peyton**
on United Shades with W. Kamau Bell on CNN

In the book, *"From the Bleachers with Love"* by David Canning Epperson, he notes, "Some sports experiences can threaten the physical, psychological, and moral well-being of your child." He advises that parents will "need to be both supportive and protective as you monitor your children's sports programs." This chapter is dedicated to assisting parents in this area because no one is going to care about your son's health and well-being more than you.

To begin, you should ensure your son has good health coverage because no youth organization, or team, is required to pay healthcare costs for their players.

If you do not have private insurance, you can apply under the Affordable Health Care Act at healthcare.gov. You can also visit insurekidsnow.gov and obtain information on free or low-cost health and dental insurance for children up to age 19.

Physical Health

There are tremendous physical benefits that come with playing basketball.

Players gain muscular endurance, learn good coordination, balance, and build their body strength. They also risk sports-related injuries that can have a substantial impact on their long-term health.

Sports injuries among young players are on the rise.

> *"Medical experts cite four key reasons for the uptick of injuries among young players: substandard sleep as a result of hectic schedules and technology use, frailer bones due to player diets being low in calcium and high sugar, specialization in basketball at early ages and weaker muscles as a result of substituting traditional weight training for more basketball optimized conditioning techniques."*[53]

In an article entitled, *These Kids are Ticking Time Bombs': The Threat of Youth Basketball,* Dr. Neeru Jayanthi, the director of sports medicine research and education at Emory, states that,

> *"Kids are broken by the time they get to college."*[54]

The NBA's medical staff and doctors have noticed the extreme wear and tear on the bodies of former AAU players. They note that "the number of games played, without training and conditioning, along with not allowing them enough time to recover, is setting them up for injuries later in their playing career."[55]

NBA Commissioner Adam Silver shared, "What our orthopedics are telling us is they're seeing wear-and-tear issues in young players that they didn't use to see until players were much older."[56]

Commissioner Silver referred to the issue as "the highest priority for the League—and I think both in terms of the health and wellness of the players in the NBA, but also the larger category of millions of players, boys and girls, not just in the United States, but globally."

LeBron James spoke to *Yahoo Sports* about the demanding schedules of AAU teams.[57]

> *"These kids are going into the league already banged up, and I think parents and coaches need to know [that] ... well, AAU coaches don't give a f—."*

He also shared,

> *"It was a few tournaments where my kids — Bronny and Bryce — had five games in one day and that's just f—ing out of control. That's just too much. And there was a case study where I read a report. I don't know who wrote it not too long ago, and it was talking about the causes and [kid's] bodies already being broken down and they contributed it to AAU basketball and how many games that these tournaments are having for the [financial benefit]. So, I'm very conscious for my own son because that's all I can control, and if my son says he's sore or he's tired, he's not playing."*

The case study is entitled, *"The NBA and Youth Basketball: Recommendations for Promoting a Healthy and Positive Experience"* by John P. Difiori, et al. published in the National Library of Medicine on pubmed.gov.

The NBA and USA Basketball have developed guidelines and accessed that "overscheduling of competitive events, overuse injuries, and burnout have become too common in youth basketball."[58] Their comprehensive guide includes scientific research, which seeks to educate parents and coaches. First and foremost, they prioritize looking out for student-athletes. The guidelines are available at youthguidelines.nba.com.

As a parent you will want to respond immediately to basketball fatigue and injuries. You should also always obtain a medical clearance for your son to return to active play. Parents should never push their

HEALTH & WELLNESS

kids beyond their physical capabilities. Nor should you allow coaches, or others, including your son, to do it either. Players may fear losing their spot on a team if they are out too long. As such, they may return too quickly while fighting and hiding their pain.

Parents should stay vigilant and explain the possible long-term consequences to their son. While others are thinking about whether Chad is healthy enough to play basketball today, I think about his future health. I do not want him to wake up at 35 years old battling injuries because of overexertion or not healing properly while he was a young athlete.

How Much Time Should Be Spent in Youth Basketball?

PLAYING SEGMENT	GAME LENGTH	GAMES PER WEEK	PRACTICE LENGTH	PRACTICES PER WEEK
Ages 7-8	20-28 minutes	1	30-60 minutes	1
Ages 9-11	24-32 minutes	1 to 2	45-75 minutes	2
Ages 12-14	28-32 minutes	2	60-90 minutes	2 to 4
Grades 9-12	32-40 minutes	2 to 3	90-120 minutes	3 to 4

Source: USA Basketball Youth Guidelines

At the collegiate level, state and federal legislators have looked to regulate college athletics in ways that add to the NCAA's recommendations concerning athlete safety.

In 2020, United States Senator Cory L. Booker (NJ) introduced S.5062 – College Athletes Bill of Rights[59] to establish health, wellness, and safety guidelines for intercollegiate athletic programs.

Unfortunately, there is no such legislation in youth basketball, so it is up to parents to keep watchful oversight. In addition, the NCAA Sports Science Institute,[60] whose mission is "to promote and develop safety, excellence, and wellness in college student-athletes, and to foster lifelong physical and mental development," is a phenomenal resource that can guide parents.

5 Health Priorities Parents Should Monitor

(1) Cardiac Health

Cardiac Health is important and woefully overlooked in youth basketball. There are reports of the tragic losses of young basketball players due to cardiac arrest. Their conditions did not show up in regular medical physicals. The key is early detection.

In 2018, during a routine physical exam, doctors found, then 18-year-old, Shareef O'Neal had a heart ailment. His mother, Shaunie Henderson, reported, "If it weren't for the doctors' discovery, he could've died from it."[61]

Shareef, who is now a spokesperson for the American Heart Association, had open-heart surgery in 2018, healed and was able to continue playing basketball.

Most medical physicals, if required at all, to play on a youth basketball team do not require cardiac testing. Unequivocally, having a player's heart checked should be a mandatory yearly requirement. Parents should have it done even if you believe your son is 100% healthy.

Health & Wellness

> *"We are here to educate others and empower others, so they hopefully don't have to suffer the loss of a child, like many of us have. I was completely blindsided by sudden cardiac arrest, and my son had had a well-child checkup the month before."*
>
> Martha-Lopez Anderson, executive director of Parent Heart Watch, whose ten-year-old son passed away while playing basketball.

Here are the types of heart screening and cardiac evaluation testing you can obtain for your son:

Electrocardiogram (ECG or EKG) measures the electrical activity of the heartbeat. It reports whether electrical activity in the heart is normal, slow, fast, or irregular. It also determines if parts of the heart are too large or are overworked.

FREE EKGs:
Parent Health Watch has locations in most states.
In Florida, young people ages 5-21 can get a free EKG test from the Nicklaus Children's Hospital.

Echocardiogram (also known as an Echo or Echocardiography) uses high-frequency sound waves (ultrasound) and takes photos of the heart's chambers, valves, walls, and the blood vessels (aorta, arteries, veins) attached to a heart. It checks how blood moves through the heart and can help diagnose heart conditions.

A **Stress Test** shows how the heart works during physical activity. This test can reveal if there are any problems with blood flow to the heart.

(2). Pulmonary Health

Pulmonary Health is for the function of the lungs and the respiratory system.

The National Research Center Network for Epidemiology and Public Health in Barcelona, Spain,[62] reports that basketball players are "a special population at risk" of chronic inflammation due to repeated injuries, frequent air travel, and immobility, among other issues. As a result, they are at risk of blood clots which can cause a ***pulmonary***

The Parent's Section: Outside The Locker Room

embolism, which is also a deadly condition. It can occur when a clot, or part of a clot, travels through the veins and ends up in the lungs.

According to the Centers for Disease Control and Protection (CDC), blood clots have also been reported as a rare side effect of the Johnson & Johnson's Janssen COVID-19 vaccine.[63]

The American Blood Clot Association reports pulmonary embolism symptoms include:[64]

- A sharp pain in the chest, particularly when taking a deep breath.
- A cough that produces blood.
- Fever.
- Dizziness.
- Rapid pulse.
- Sudden shortness of breath.
- Unexplained sweating.

There are two types of pulmonary tests:

A ***spirometry test*** is a basic lung test that is recommended if there is any wheezing, shortness of breath, or a cough. This is also the same test that diagnoses asthma or chronic obstructive pulmonary disease (COPD). It measures how much air is inhaled, how much air is exhaled, and how quickly you exhale. The second is a ***CT angiography test*** which checks for blood clots in the head, neck, chest, or abdomen.

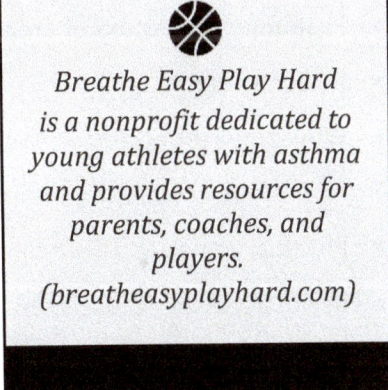

Breathe Easy Play Hard is a nonprofit dedicated to young athletes with asthma and provides resources for parents, coaches, and players. (breatheasyplayhard.com)

Asthma and Sports-Induced Asthma

Asthma affects 25 million people in the United States,[65] including those with sports or exercise-induced asthma. With effective management, many still live an active life and achieve their athletic dreams.

The National Athletic Trainers Association (NATA) states, "As many as 15%-25% of all athletes have signs or symptoms of asthma." They

HEALTH & WELLNESS

also report, "it is something that is developed over time and can be limited, or completely disappear." [66]

Several current and former NBA players have asthma, including James Harden (Philadelphia 76ers).

According to the NATA, the major signs of asthma are:

- Chest tightness (in children, it is chest pain).
- Coughing (especially at night).
- An athlete who is well-conditioned but does not seem to be able to perform at a level comparable to other athletes who do not have asthma.
- Prolonged shortness of breath (dyspnea).
- Difficulty sleeping.
- Wheezing (especially after exercise).
- Inability to catch one's breath.
- Physical activities affected by breathing difficulty.
- Use of accessory muscles to breathe.
- Breathing difficulty upon awakening in the morning.
- Breathing difficulty when exposed to certain allergens or irritants.
- Exercise-induced symptoms, such as coughing or wheezing.
- Family history of asthma.
- Personal history of atopy (allergies such as eczema or hay fever).

Sports-Induced Asthma (SIA), also known as Exercise-Induced Bronchoconstriction (EIB), occurs when airways are constricted during physical activity.

According to the American College of Allergy, Asthma, & Immunology (ACCAI), 90% of people with asthma have EIB, but not everyone with EIB has asthma. As such many people misinterpret it.

Many elite and world-class athletes have EIB, including DeAndre Jordan (Denver Nuggets). Fortunately, many athletes are able to stay active and symptom free.

For college players, the NCAA allows asthma medications, such as inhalers, with a prescription and documentation.

Three useful resources for asthma management are:

- *"What Athletes Need to Know About Inhaled Medications"* from the U.S. Anti-Doping Agency under their FAQs at USADA.org.
- The *Asthma Action Plan* from the U.S. Department of Health and Human Services and the National Heart Lung and Blood institute at acaai.org.
- The Mayo Clinic (mayoclinic.org.)

(3) Injuries: Fractures and Bone Health

"Almost one-third of all injuries incurred in childhood are sports-related injuries."[67]

Parents should be aware that practices are more dangerous than games. According to a report by Yale Medicine entitled, *Kids' Sports Injuries: What Parents Need to Know* by Kathy Katella,

> *"Sixty-two percent of organized sports-related injuries happen during practice, not during a game or competition."*

In addition, this current generation of basketball players are cautioned against playing full throttle on concrete courts because of the injury risk.

Use ICE for **muscle pain and stiffness**.
For **sprains**, use the "RICE" treatment: Rest, Ice, Compression, and Elevation.

Use HEAT for acute injuries or pain, along **with inflammation and swelling**.

Keep Your Medicine Cabinet Stocked with:
Non-inflammatory medicines (Advil)
Ace Bandages
Band-Aids
Alcohol
Peroxide

Health & Wellness

Injuries affect recruitment and loss of playing time at every level of basketball. Joel Embiid (Philadelphia 76ers) had to sit out his first two seasons due to fractures found just days before the 2014 NBA draft.[68] Stress fractures in the feet have also stopped the careers of NBA Hall of Famers Bill Walton and Yao Ming.[69]

The most common injuries in basketball are sprained ankles, foot fractures, knee injuries such as ACL tears, jammed fingers, facial cuts, and deep thigh bruises. Players may also experience injuries to their teeth. Minor injuries like pulled muscles and sprains are easily managed by a physician. If there are a foot or leg injuries (or any other injury that requires hospitalization or rehabilitation therapy), or if a physician recommends surgery, you should seriously consider a specialist to provide a second opinion.

As one basketball parent relayed to me anonymously,

> *"When my son was recruited, coming off of a fracture, my first question to his coaches and staff was how would they treat the injured foot to ensure no further damage throughout his playing career? I got several different answers from the team's doctor's to the trainers."*

(4) Bone Density

Basketball players possess a higher bone mineral density than other athletes. It is important to monitor their vitamin D levels because many basketball players are reported to be deficient. You should also monitor calcium levels to ensure optimal bone health.

The Orthopedic Sports Journal of Medicine reports 32.3% of NBA combine participants from 2009-2013 had vitamin D deficiencies.[70]

Over 73% of NBA players identify as Black, and the study also reports, "Dark skin pigmentation is a known risk factor for vitamin D insufficiency. The increased melanin found in the skin of darkly pigmented individuals may increase the amount of time to synthesize vitamin D up to 10-fold."

Growth Spurts and Osgood-Schlatter Disease

Most basketball players are taller than average and some may have gone through a growth spurt.

Parents should watch out for **Osgood-Schlatter**, a disease that affects 200,000 people per year and kids during growth spurts.[71] It is caused by repetitive activities in growing teenagers and causes a painful lump in the kneecaps. The good news is that physicians report it usually resolves on its own once the bones stop growing (usually between 14 and 18 years old).

If you are curious about the potential height of your child, some pediatric orthopedic surgeons believe they can estimate when a child's growth is completed by determining their "bone age." Although whether it works is debatable by some physicians, the procedure is done by x-raying the left wrist. The x-ray will ascertain which growth plates are still open, and that will determine the expected height.

Two physicians from the University of Maryland created the app, "Multiplier" which they claim can predict a child's height. It is available on Google Play and Apple.

(5) Exercise Heat Exhaustion (EHS)

EHS is one of the top three causes of sudden death in athletes.[72]

Playing in hot gyms is a part of the youth basketball world. I have been in a few, even in the dead heat of summer.

As a parent, let your son know that if he ever gets too hot, he should immediately stop playing.

The first signs of heat exhaustion include heavy sweating, headache, nausea, dizziness, weakness, irritability, thirst, and irritability. The fastest way to recover is to rest in a cool place, drink something cold, and loosen any clothing.

HEALTH & WELLNESS

Questions to ask a coach on a new team.

1. What medical personnel is available for the team during games?
2. Do you, or your staff, know CPR?
3. Does the gym/facility have a defibrillator?
4. Is there water available at games and practice?
5. Is there an on-site emergency plan?
6. Are medical evaluations or clearances required?
7. What is your COVID vaccination policy?

Mental Health Wellness: *"They Forget We Are Kids."*

> *"What people don't understand is, even the writers and stuff, if they have children of their own. Imagine if somebody talked about their child how they spoke about me. Critiquing my body, critiquing how I look. Every time they talked about me, it was about weight, how bad I looked. I don't even think they realized what kind of impact that can have on you."*[73]
> Zion Williamson (New Orleans Pelicans)

One day I overheard a group conversation with Chad and his teammates. One of them, was a highly sought-after college recruit, who shared his dismay at having to speak with so many reporters during his college recruitment. He complained that he did not have much time for himself. Chad and the others were giving him words of encouragement and telling him how lucky he was.

He sadly replied, "I know, but sometimes they forget we are kids."

It was a shocking revelation for me, but true. I got chills and realized that mental wellness is a huge part of basketball and youth athletics. You can see from online commentary that adults have little regard for the mental and psychological turmoil they may be inflicting on young athletes. And since they do not seem to care, parents must make sure it is their priority every step of the way.

Some parents may believe their son would be lucky to have reporters after him, but parents must understand that basketball is a mental game as much as a physical one. Players must be able to quiet their thoughts so instinct can take over, which transposes into their off the court lives.

Their attitudes also shape their performance, academically *and* emotionally. Players pursuing their basketball dreams can rarely "turn off" basketball, and everyone wants to talk basketball with them.

In addition, unless you are tall, you also have no idea how irritating it is that almost every day, extra-tall people are approached by strangers

HEALTH & WELLNESS

because of our height. The first thing someone will say, even before saying hello is, "Wow, you're tall." Or they ask, "How tall are you?"

Then they ask, "Do you play basketball?"

Or they joke, "How's the air up there?"

It is annoying.

Anyone who speaks with Chad and other tall young players rarely ask about them as a person or a student. Coaches may ask them, "How are your grades?" but not "What's your major?"

Girls in high school may tease them for their above-average height. They get to college, and things change. Now the young women may flirt with them. Your son may wonder if he is being liked for who he is as a person or because he is on the basketball team.

They may look for love in all the wrong places from anyone who gives them attention. After a while, they may only see themselves as a jock.

Players may also have unrealistic expectations placed upon them to win regardless of anything happening in their lives off the court. There may be issues in their home life that they cannot share with others. Some may not have parents coming to see them play, and no one is cheering for them.

Far too many have to pretend everything is okay, even if it is not.

They are expected to balance so much on their own. Workouts, school studies, and relations with their teammates and coaches while smiling and always trying to keep the best demeanor toward others. Some players use the gym to get away from their life's battles.

After a game, by the time a parent leaves the gym, your son is likely already reliving the game in his head and mentally preparing for the next. These are more issues outside the locker room. Just thinking about them exhausts me, even as a seasoned adult.

Young athletes struggle, and many keep a lot bottled up inside. Check on the ones who always seem to be grinning or exhibit nervous laughter,

The Parent's Section: Outside The Locker Room

which is an incongruous emotion. The laughter is likely helping them heal from trauma.

Kevin Love (Cleveland Cavaliers), a five-time All-Star, a two-time member of the All-NBA Second Team who also won an NBA championship with the Cleveland Cavaliers, publicly shared his personal experience after having a pre-game panic attack.

In 2018, he wrote a heart-wrenching article entitled *"Everyone is Going Through Something:"*[74]

> *"I was 20 or 21 years old, and I'd grown up around basketball. And on basketball teams. Nobody talked about what they were struggling with on the inside. I remember thinking, what are my problems? I'm healthy. I play basketball for a living. What do I have to worry about?*
> *I'd never heard of any pro athlete talking about mental health, and I didn't want to be the only one. I didn't want to look weak. Honestly, I just didn't think I needed it. It's like the playbook said — figure it out on your own, like everyone else around me always had."*

That year, he established the Kevin Love Fund to help people improve their physical and emotional well-being. His noteworthy plan is to help one billion people!

Other professional players have publicly shared their battles with self-doubt and what it took to overcome it. Former NBA Player Dwayne Brown, who currently plays in France, spoke of his depression:

> *"My first two years [in the NBA] I dealt with depression. Not playing – in my head—Am I good enough? So, coming over here...being a factor, being one of the main guys, that made me feel so good."*[75]

The pressure to succeed at basketball and/or to get any accolades, including a scholarship, is often overwhelming to a young player. They

Health & Wellness

may experience burnout, anxiety, and depression. They are expected to be unbreakable in an environment that makes their struggle unique from their peers. They are expected to maintain "mental toughness," although coaches may punish them when they make mistakes on the court.

Trainers push them hard to get maximum results. Their peers may tease their performance. Parents may add unwarranted pressure. Nutritionists are changing their eating habits. Teachers are on them about their schoolwork. They get up early and go to bed late. Online keyboard warriors, and armchair critics, comment openly about them. Reporters and sports analysts probe.

Allyson Wynn, whose son Will Thomas plays for Morgan State, says,

> *"It's easy for a coach to excuse a player to see the trainer to treat an injury he or she can see with a trained eye. But who treats the mental disorders that athletic staff can't, won't, or don't see that have bigger impacts on academic and athletic performance?"*

Another college basketball parent shared, on the condition of anonymity,

> *"When I asked what was in place to treat my son's recovery from anxiety and depression, I got crickets from most. I was encouraged to have him stay in touch with his private psychiatrist. There seems to be no value or emphasis on caring for the mental health of young athletes."*

Suicidal tendencies are also something college recruiting staff look out for. Colleges are now offering more on-campus mental health services to student-athletes.

Some believe there is a mental health crisis in sports.

In the first five months of 2022, five young athletes from various sports committed suicide.[76] The social isolation that canceled seasons during the pandemic also contributed to heightened stress among athletes.

Although many are now publicly advocating for mental health awareness in sports, there is still a stigma attached. Young people, whether they play basketball or not, should not have to be embarrassed or suffer alone if they are facing mental health challenges. This is where parents, family, spiritual/religious leaders, and mental health professionals are vital.

Parents should take time out of their day to have non-basketball related discussions with their sons. Ask about their friends and check on their foes. Ask them how they are feeling overall and whether everything is okay? Advise your son to get help even if they are not in a crisis. Encourage them to get a hobby and do non-basketball activities.

Text them encouraging quotes and recommend books, YouTube videos, or podcasts that relax the mind and soul. Plan getaways or outings, even if it is only for a few hours.

Chad and I have an annual "Mom and Son-day" where at least one Sunday a year, we do something unique together. We cannot discuss "anything basketball." I also treat my kids to spa days, and because Chad is a low-key comedian, we always send each other the most hilarious videos from social media.

If you are a Believer, you can also gift them with a Bible or another Holy Book. One of my best friends, Wallis Etienne, gifted Chad a monogrammed Bible this past year, and he cherishes it.

You can also share a Bible quote that inspires me.

> **"When you go through deep waters,**
> **I will be with you."**
> **—Isaiah 43:2**

If your son needs help with his mental (or emotional) health, you should, without reservation, seek a therapist, including a sports psychologist or sports psychiatrist, who has more knowledge of the struggles of an athlete.

Health & Wellness

DeMar DeRozan (Chicago Bulls), who has a base salary of $27.3 million, also struggles with depression. DeRozan says he does not believe he will ever be "truly happy" until he retires.

He wants others to know, "One should never be ashamed of wanting to be a better you."[77]

Let your son know that talking about his feelings, whatever they may be, is normal and that you will always be there for him. You can keep it confidential and only share it with coaches and others if that is what you and your son decide.

Without any doubt, I am thoroughly convinced,

> *"America needs a national symposium on youth basketball and the monopoly before college."*

One with players "on the podium" sharing their viewpoint and proposing ideas to compliment what caring adults are already doing.

Adult financial motives have fueled a change in youth basketball. It seems the interest of young people is lost. We are not doing enough for student-athletes.

Zachary Hollywood (1998-2017), who played at Ball State, committed suicide at 17 years old. His last Tweet, posted the morning he took his life, is a message for humanity, but especially for the adults who control the youth basketball world:

> *"Be careful what you say to everyone because you don't know what kind of battles they are going through."*

Mental Health Resources

- *Protecting Youth Mental Health* - A 2021 report by the U.S. Surgeon General's Advisory can be found at hhs.gov.

- How Youth Sports Leaders Can Support the Mental Health of Their Players (leagueapps.com)

- TrueSport provides a comprehensive website with videos, downloadable resources, and apps. (truesport.org)
- U.S. Center for Mental Health & Sport (mentalhealthandsport.org)
- Speakingofsuicide.com
- National Suicide Prevention Hotline: 988 or 800-273-TALK (8255) (988lifeline.org)
- Crisis Text Line – Text HOME to 741741

Pain Management and Medication

Managing pain is a part of an athlete's life, and they will likely experience it at some point. The American Academy of Pediatrics (aap.org) offers guidance for young athletes and advises that "Pain medicines can be used to treat acute injuries. However, in some cases, pain relief can mask important warning signs and lead to further injury."

At some point, your son may be prescribed opioids (oxycodone, hydrocodone, or morphine) to help with pain after an injury or surgery. Opioids can lead to addiction, so parents have to be watchful.

The U.S. Department of Health and Human Services (HHS) reported that "10.3 million people ages 12 and older misused prescription opioids in 2018."[78]

The National Survey on Drug Use and Health reports that opioid misuse is 50% higher in kids participating in high-injury sports, such as basketball.

As your son gets closer to his college years, you may want to review the list of the NCAA "banned substances"[79] and, if needed, information on how to request and receive "medical exception procedures" from the NCAA. I was surprised to learn that excessive use of caffeine is prohibited.

Parents should also be mindful of any medication prescribed by a psychiatrist for their short-and long-term effects on them as athletes.

Parents can also visit Connect2Prevent (nsc.org) to find discussion guides on pain management.

Harmful Drug Usage: Marijuana and Fentanyl

The most used drugs among U.S. teenagers are marijuana, painkillers, and prescription drugs such as Percocet.

Marijuana usage adversely affects the developing brains of young people. The CDC reports,

> *"Marijuana use might have permanent effects on the developing brain when usage begins in adolescence, especially with regular or heavy use. Teens who use marijuana are more likely to quit high school or not get a college degree."*[80]

They also report that those who are addicted "may also be at a higher risk of other negative consequences, such as problems with attention, memory, and learning."

The CDC shares that athletes claim to use marijuana "for relief of anxiety and stress, and perhaps to reduce muscle spasms. "Several studies have also linked marijuana use to increased risk for psychiatric disorders, including psychosis (schizophrenia), depression, anxiety, and substance use disorders.

Smoking high-potency marijuana daily could increase the chances of developing psychosis by nearly five times compared to people who have never used marijuana.[81] Many people do not know that smoking it regularly can also cause psychotic episodes in people predisposed to it.

Generation Z is full of many young people with psychiatric issues due to the use of cannabis in some form. They refer to it as "tweaking." Some basketball players' careers have been thwarted because of marijuana use. Its usage, along with synthetic cannabinoids, is banned by the NCAA for college players.

Pharmaceutical fentanyl, which can be legally obtained through a prescription, is a synthetic opioid used for pain.

Law enforcement agencies are reporting fentanyl abuse among teenagers is also on the rise, and it is being mixed into marijuana. "Teen overdose deaths have never been higher in the U.S. as young Americans are increasingly poisoned by the synthetic opiate fentanyl."[82]

In addition, Spice (or K2), a synthetic marijuana and stimulant used to treat attention-deficit hyperactivity disorder (ADHD) (e.g., Adderall and Ritalin), is also considered harmful.

Marijuana is a "downer" substance. Athletes need clarity and energy. They do not need to go into deep internal thoughts because it can make them overthink situations and make them paranoid. The relaxation, or stress relief young athletes who may smoke marijuana believe they are obtaining is a façade. No student-athlete should ever use harmful drugs, nor should they risk being around others who are using it.

Nutritional Health

At 6'10 and 270 pounds, my son is the tallest and the strongest man in the history of our lineage—a fact I am proud of, especially since Chad was a natural childbirth.

Many had us believing that because of his height, he would automatically receive a scholarship. When Chad was in the 11th grade, and we were trying to ascertain why he was not receiving college offers, a former NBA player shared that Chad was not passing the athleticism eye test. He told us Chad lacked "the look" of the average basketball player which is tall and slim. During his freshman year in college, Coach Brian Merritt, a former assistant coach at Morgan State, helped Chad lose over 60 pounds. Other coaches and family members were astonished.

Chad still works out with vigor and is changing not just his diet, but his lifestyle as it pertains to eating. He must keep the weight off and stay in top basketball shape and healthy. Coaches can be very tough in this area. Everyone must have the same "look," regardless of how they perform on the court.

My son motivated me so much to take care of my own health, I genuinely believe he should share his regiment with others on YouTube.

Health & Wellness

I learned that as parents of athletes, we could learn by example how to eat healthier, exercise, and care for our own health.

High school basketball players ages 17-19 burn around 3,000-5,000 calories per day,[83] and their diet should be high in carbohydrates and low in fat. They should eat whole grains, fruits, vegetables, and milk to maximize their vitamin and mineral intake. Good meat choices are lead red meat, skinless poultry, and seafood.

The Gatorade Sports Institute's *"Fueling the Basketball Athlete: The Practitioner's Approach"* and *"Vegetarian and Vegan Diets for Athletic Training and Performance"* provides nutritional information, including sample meal plans and recommendations on what to eat pre- and post-games.

How To Eat Healthy Before A Basketball Game by USA Basketball is also a good source of information. Surprisingly, the best fruits to eat before a game are watermelon, oranges, cantaloupe, and grapes.

Fast Food

The reality is that young people love fast food. No matter how many home-cooked meals a parent may make, players will eat outside, especially when traveling.

However, not all fast food is bad.

According to New York City's Hospital for Special Surgery,[84] the following fast foods are good for athletes:

- Thick crust pizza, which provides lots of carbohydrates, and the cheese provides needed calcium.
- Burgers with extra tomatoes and lettuce without any sauce.
- Skinless roasted or grilled chicken.
- Pasta (spaghetti or noodles with meat/poultry/vegetables).
- Chili and hearty soups.
- Salads offer healthy meals high in carbohydrates.

- Deli sandwiches, wraps, and pita sandwiches filled with vegetables, meat, or cheese. Sandwiches made with whole grain bread will provide needed fiber.

Sexual and Other Abuse in Sports

Sexual abuse is rampant in youth sports and goes significantly underreported. It impacts an estimated 2%-8% of all student-athletes under 18 and even more college athletes.[85]

> *More than 1 in 4 current or former student-athletes reported being sexually assaulted or harassed by someone in a position of power on campus, such as their coaches and trainers, and nearly half feared that their perpetrator would retaliate against them.[86]*

The U.S. Center for SafeSport, whose mission is "to investigate and end abuse in sports," reports that compared with other races and sexual orientations, Black athletes and bisexual athletes experience nearly double the rates of inappropriate sexual touching. [87]

Parents should discuss sexual and other abuse with their sons and be watchful.

When Chad was still a teenager, he had tryouts for a team in a neighboring state. The coach sent an Uber for him and a team member (Chad's friend that lived nearby). Afterward, without anyone asking my permission, the coach took them to his house. Chad called excitedly to share how he was getting ready to play on the coach's indoor basketball court. I was skeptical because the coach had not mentioned it earlier when we spoke about Chad coming to the tryout. I put enthusiasm in my voice and said, "Wow, an indoor court! Okay, have fun and text me the address."

After a few hours, Chad called to ask whether he could spend the night.

"This kid is pushing it," I thought. Telling him no was easy.

Health & Wellness

Like an attorney, Chad began to argue his case.

He told me his friend had stayed over all the time, and there was more than enough room.

My kids know me pretty well, and before I could get the sentence out, Chad relayed, "Coach said to call him."

He quickly added, "You know I am not going to let anyone do anything bad to me, right?"

Instead of calling the coach first, I called his friend's mother. I learned she had never met the coach, either. That solidified my decision that he would not be staying the night. I then called the coach and Chad to let them know.

I am not alleging there would have been any abuse of Chad, sexually or otherwise. I just did not like the way it played out. I believe adults should always speak with other adults when minor children are in their care. That is the way I was raised. Yet, it is not an expected courtesy for parents in youth basketball. Parents are expected to trust anyone, and everyone, who has a coaching title or is affiliated with a basketball organization. And they do. No questions asked.

One only needs to Google "coaches who abused basketball players" or "sexual abuse in basketball" to learn that my worrying was not far-fetched. There are so many horror stories that I grew tired of scrolling. However, one recent story stood out to me.

In July 2022, a *Des Moines Register* article entitled, *"You forced evil... upon my son,"*[88] details the horrific crimes of Greg Stephen.

Stephen, who was referred to as a "longtime AAU coach," was sentenced to 180 years (1-8-0) years in prison because he "collected [nude] images and videos of more than 400 (4-0-0) boys over two decades." He was also convicted of "physically molesting more than a dozen boys." His victims were awarded $1 million as part of a class-action lawsuit.

In sports, it is typical and harmless behavior for coaches to smack a player's rear end as a term of endearment for a good job. It does not seem to bother "the boys" at all. I always cringed when I saw a grown man do that to my son. I have helped countless minors who have been victims of unthinkable sexual abuse, even from their own parents. That trauma is life-changing, and many never recover.

Moms Team (momsteam.com), who provides resources for sports parents, recommends the following to thwart sexual abuse in sports:

1. Two-Adult Rule. Make sure your child is never alone with an adult.
2. Inquire whether a team conducts background checks [or run one yourself].
3. Learn the warning signs, such as special attention from a coach or one who is trying to be a surrogate parent.
4. Try and notice if your son is suddenly missing practices, has a loss of interest, withdrawing, or performing less? Are they angry or sad all the time? These are telltale signs of abuse.
5. Get to know the leaders of the organization. Search their online accounts and view their social media posts, and their connections.
6. Teach your children to distinguish between proper and improper touching.

Other Abuse

Abuse in sports is not only sexual, but it can also be physical and mental as well.

The story of Marlon Dorsey, a former high school coach in Jackson, MS, is an example. In 2010, Dorsey was videotaped beating a player with a weight-lifting belt.[89] Dorsey, who played at Mississippi State and Oklahoma State, was also accused of calling players "weak" and "sissy."

In his apology letter, Dorsey stated, "I took it upon myself to save these young men from the destruction of self and what society has accepted and become silent to the issues our students are facing on a daily basis." Dorsey also explained that his course of discipline was "for their own good."

Health & Wellness

Their parents disagreed and sued the school district.

Dorsey apologized and said, "I am deeply remorseful of my actions to help our students."

Even to the end, Dorsey thought he was "helping."

How to Report Abuse

The Safe Sport Authorization Act of 2017 requires amateur sports organizations "to report sexual abuse allegations immediately to local or federal law enforcement, or a child agency designated by the U.S. Justice Department."[90]

Parents can document it first and then present it to the superintendent of schools, the principal/headmaster, the state board of education, the governing athletic association, and request they pass it on to law enforcement.

For grassroots teams, including AAU, it is recommended that it is immediately reported to law enforcement. The AAU also has a mandatory reporting policy for its employees and volunteers should they witness abuse. Parents should communicate and let their sons know they should come to them concerning any, or all, suspect behavior. They should also ask if anyone is threatening to take away their playing time or remove them from a team "if they tell…"

Check on your son if you have any "gut" feelings or notice anything strange. Abuse *is* a real part of youth sports—pay attention.

CHAPTER VII

Branding & Making Money

"The high school locker room is arguably the last bastion of amateurism within an education-based setting, and we want to protect that. The purpose of high school athletics is very different from the professional level – and even the college level.
High school students can enjoy some success with NIL, but it cannot be done while wearing the school uniform."

— Dr. Karissa Niehoff, CEO,
National Federation of State High School Associations

Name, Image, and Likeness (NIL)

In July 2021, the NCAA began allowing college athletes to make money using their "name, image, and likeness" (NIL). This means a student-athlete can earn money through personal branding and selling merchandise, which includes autographs, making personal appearances, promoting a business, social media endorsements, and video game representations.

Once the college ruling was implemented, conversations began on whether high school students could do the same. The answer is yes, depending upon the state they live in.

BRANDING & MAKING MONEY

NILs give players unimaginable economic opportunities and can be ideal for high school players who cannot work during the summer or get part-time jobs, or internships, like other young people.

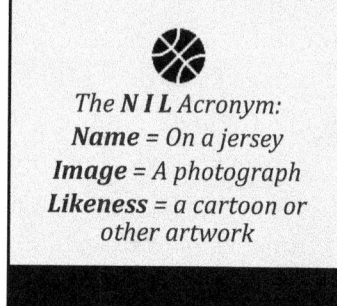

The **N I L** Acronym:
Name = On a jersey
Image = A photograph
Likeness = a cartoon or other artwork

NIL deals are obtained in numerous ways, including players being hired by representatives from corporations and retail stores. Sports agents, who are now allowed to represent high school players, are also reaching out to players and their parents.

Privately-owned NIL firms promising to connect student-athletes to money-making opportunities are forming and marketing heavily to players.

Parents and players seeking opportunities should protect themselves:

- You can review a list of the high school and college NIL rules online at on3.com and ncaa.com.

- Never sign any NIL contract/agreement without an attorney review.

- Make sure no one will control your son's full name, his nickname, a trade name, or any logo associated with him that he would like to keep for his exclusive use. A company tried to give Chad a contract where, had he signed, they would have owned his name for life.

Mikey Williams, Johnuel Flands (Archbishop Stepinac; and, Ian Jackson (Cardinal Hayes) were the first high school players to sign a NIL deal in New York City.
Source: One37PM.com

The Parent's Section: Outside The Locker Room

- Watch out for agreements that have the word "perpetual" or similar phrases which may mean "forever."
- Players must check with their coach and athletic director before executing any NIL agreement. Some high school associations prohibit high school players from earning revenue while playing.

Luke Fedlam, Esq. my colleague over at the College Basketball Parent's Association (CBPA) and managing partner and founder of Advance (advancenil.com), an organization dedicated to NIL opportunities notes, "Paid activities cannot be affiliated with the student-athletes' high school."[91] In other words, high school students cannot promote any service or product in their uniforms. They also cannot do photoshoots on school property.

Parents can also help create entrepreneurial opportunities. You can encourage your son to ask local businesses if he can promote them. He can create his own branded merchandise and use drop shipping to sell it online. He can also try monetizing his social media, building a digital fan base, or offering autographs for money.

Coach Tony Hargraves relayed to me,

> *"A high school player with a NIL deal will likely be highly attractive to a college coach seeking new recruits. If that player is already generating publicity in his hometown, the likelihood it will benefit a college will bring added value."*

However, players are cautioned against entering into agreements in which a college coach or recruiter may offer NIL deals to convince players to attend or transfer to their college. This type of relationship is an NCAA violation and jeopardizes college eligibility.

The NCAA is even asking for help from member institutions to report violations and stated in a letter to them:

> *"We also constantly reviewing new reports of tampering, recruiting inducements, impermissible benefits, impermissible recruiters and other related behaviors."*[92]

BRANDING & MAKING MONEY

If your son does go the NIL route, he may be able to deduct sports-related expenses against his income. You may also consider creating an LLC for tax purposes and hiring a certified public accountant. You can also set up a foundation or donate money to charities, which also provide tax benefits.

NIL Opportunities and Support

- *David McGriff, Esq.*, is a Los Angeles-based attorney representing NIL clients. His son, Quincy McGriff plays for Duquesne. McGriff is available to review potential contracts and help protect student-athlete's names and brands. His tweets on NIL subjects (@the_nil_lawyer) are a worthy resource for parents and players. Website: thenilllawyer.com

- *Team Altemus* (team-altemus.com), founded by Courtney Altemus, offers comprehensive NIL information for student-athletes and athletic departments.

- *NILcollegeathletes.com* has a database with deals, companies, athletes, and agents.

- *Sqwad* (sqwadhq.com) has a sports sponsorship price calculator that can estimate how much to charge for sponsorships based on social media counts.

- *The Business of College Sports* (businessofcollegesports.com), founded by Kristi Dosh, an attorney and sports analyst for ESPN, is a site that keeps up with the NIL marketplace for athletes.

- *The National Federation of State High School Associations (NFSHA)* provides a free NIL course at nfhslearn.com.

Although NIL opportunities are currently benefitting more college students than those in high school, we will likely see more opportunities for them as we move into a new era for student-athletes.

Online Exposure and Social Media

A player can seek to build their name (or brand) off the court using these online resources: **Google Knowledge Panel, Wikipedia, and Wikidata.** *On Google Alerts,* he can sign up, and whenever his name is mentioned online (e.g., in a news article or blog post), he will receive an email notification with a link.

Social Media: College coaches cannot find your son if they do not know him. The more your son posts, the more people will view him online. This will increase his chances of appearing in online searches when grassroots, or college coaches, look for recruits. If your son scores during a game, post it. You both should post and share his highlight videos, workout videos, photos, awards, NIL opportunities, and news stories. Create a hashtag of his name and add it to every post with his uniform number (e.g., #ChadVenning32) and the team's name (e.g., #TeamRams). Large social media followings also are a direct correlation to lucrative NIL deals.

Be cautious about social media postings.

Today's generation makes posts to get clout, impress their peers, and earn revenue. Some will need an adult to help them discern what may be improper. Explain to your son that not only will a coach worry about a player making him/her look bad, but a corporation or a retail store will also. Let them know the risks of being a part of any online controversy, even if is only perceived, can still hurt him.

For example, many young people like to pose with hand gestures. Members of my generation (Generation X) and Baby Boomers may perceive them as gang signs. And since many corporate leaders, college coaches, and other decision-makers are likely from the same generations, it may be easily misconstrued. It also should be obvious that posting, or even reposting, any violence, weapons, drugs, or sexual content will be a negative blight.

On a regular basis, many coaches publicly share that they have passed over recruits after checking their social media. Not only are

Branding & Making Money

players losing scholarship opportunities because of social media, but they may also lose the chance to earn money.

Highlight Videos, Photos, and Media Interviews

Chad once had a teammate whose father filmed every one of his son's games since he was in elementary school. He came to games with a small production set-up complete with lighting. He was smart and probably knew that video footage would come in handy later.

Highlight videos are 2-5 minutes of video clips that capture overall talent and player ability on the court.

Your son should have an errorless highlight video which will be used in the college recruiting process as a visual resume. They may also be useful for NIL opportunities and to get recruited on grassroots teams.

Highlight videos should not be confused with a mixtape video, which is more promotional and may include music. Mixtapes are used primarily for social media entertainment and promotion.

In youth basketball, someone may be filming your son, especially at tournaments. If a videographer makes a highlight video of your son, it is fair to assume they are an above-average player. You can also pay someone to create a highlight video for your son. If you decide to make them yourself, Adobe Premier Pro and Final Cut Pro X are software products used by the pros.

The following companies have made resourceful videos of Chad and posted them on their social media, which helped. I cannot thank them enough. Please see whether they would be a good resource for your son.

- **City Outworks** (cityoutworks.com) AAU members receive a discount on highlight videos. They also offer YouTube and Instagram posts.
- **The Hoop Hustle** (thehoophustle.com)
  Twitter: @TheHoopHustle
- **Visionary Vizuals** on Instagram @vizvizuals

Photos

For a long time, I remember when the photos I took were all we had. Chad would tease me about my photography skills but appreciated the effort. Then one day, professionals were covering Chad.

However, purchasing photos can be costly. The Associated Press (AP) and Getty Images have phenomenal shots of Chad when he played in the NBA HBCU Classic. AP offered me a discounted rate of $125 for one photo, and the Getty Images' cost was $1,405 for a 10-year license.

Most self-employed photographers, who cover youth sports, will allow you to repost their photos or even use them professionally at no cost. Just remember to give them credit.

Nicole Sweet covers youth basketball and takes phenomenal photographs. She advertises that she is "only a flight away" and is one of the few women I have ever seen covering youth basketball. You can reach her on Instagram @nicolesweetsports. Website: nicolesweetphoto.com.

Jon Lopez is another one of my favorites. He states in his bio, "My jump shot didn't get me to the league, so my snapshot did." You can reach him on Instagram @jonlopez13.

MaxPreps (maxpreps.com) advertises a photographers' network for high school sports.

Parents should be aware that a photographer can use their child's photos without consent, and they own the rights to them. The exception is in Georgia, where no one can photograph a minor without the consent of a parent or guardian.[93] It should also be understood that no photographs can be used for sexual or predatory purposes, which violates child pornography laws. Parents should get in the habit of doing regular internet searches for photos, and any videos, of their student-athlete.

Media Interviews

Once a player receives notoriety, reporters will want to speak with him. You should practice media interviews with your son.

You should also remind your son that the camera and microphones are "always on." They should always be mindful of what they say or do, outside of the locker room—especially when sitting on the bench.

The press can be an effective and positive tool when handled correctly. It can be a nightmare when it is not.

Coaches will likely instruct their players on how to handle controversial situations. If they do not, you can tell your son his best response is "No comment." He should then direct the reporter to a team or school leader.

Here are two great resources which may help prepare for media interviews:

- *"Interview Techniques and Interactions for Quinnipac [University] Student-Athletes"* on gobobcats.com

- *"13 Ways to Give A Great Media Interview"* at Via Sport (viasport.ca).

CHAPTER VIII

Going Pro

"So do not worry about tomorrow; tomorrow will worry about itself. Each day has enough trouble of its own."
— Matthew 6:34

That Bible reference is fitting for any young person wondering what adulthood may offer them. In every step of his basketball journey, Chad spent an inordinate amount of time worrying about what was next. He wanted to know whether he would play professionally. What is the plan if he could no longer play? What is his best career path with a business degree?

It is more than likely that your son may have similar questions.

When most seasoned adults were in our late teens, or early twenties, many of us did not have a clue as to what we would do for a living either.

One step at a time is what I tell Chad.

The statistics on advancing in basketball to college on a scholarship or to the professional level, may seem grim to young players. Only 1.2% of NCAA players make the jump to the NBA. It can place self-doubt on some. For others, it becomes their motivation.

What is missing from that equation is not all professional players go through the NCAA college route. Attending college is not the only option for a young player who wants to play professionally in the NBA or in another league. However, every young basketball player should have a contingency plan, just like any other high school or college graduate. I also believe all young players who have dreams to play professionally should share the sentiment of Jay Z who once said, "I am not a businessman, I am a business man."

Parents and players must stay methodical, realistic, hopeful, and professional. Since the future cannot be predicted, I also let Chad know to live in the present and to embrace his journey. I am also a firm believer that one should not worry about things that have not yet happened.

Tomorrow will take care of itself.

While Chad took care of what he needed to do academically and on the court, I segmented youth basketball to help him off the court. One of my cousins joked that I had turned into a "Momanager" and a pseudo-Tasha Mack, the fictional character from the comedy-drama series, *The Game*. Mack's character, played by Wendy Raquel Robinson, is the mother and savvy sports agent to a fictional NFL player. That is pretty extreme, but youth basketball is filled with mothers in similar positions.

When Chad played AAU, I kept up with grassroots basketball and the circuit. I knew the coaches, the teams, the tournaments, the rules, and how his participation would make an impact.

It was the same when he played in high school. I followed high school tournaments, college recruiting events, the NCAA regulations, helped him focus on his academics, and researched other players in his position for upcoming games. And although all through high school, he considered himself a forward and was training to be one, I sent him countless articles and videos on great centers which is now benefitting him greatly in college and his conference.

Besides Coach Rivera at his prep school, no other coach Chad played for had viable conversations with us about college basketball recruitment or beyond. Most focused on his current situation and his usefulness at the time. When he played well, they told us he had a shot. When he had a bad game, they left him on his own.

Chad was also helped by other coaches, even though he may have never worked out with them or played on their team. If a coach ever called me about Chad, they always shared that they would be available to help if they could. Parents use all of your resources and the network.

Now that Chad is in college, I know the college "circuit." The only high school players I know about are the ones that are heavily promoted in the media or on my Twitter feed. I have become an NCAA pundit, and for the first time in decades I now watch college basketball. The arenas are tremendously larger than those for youth basketball games. The fans come for entertainment, to support their college and players. For many colleges, winning championships means millions in revenue and huge financial bonuses for coaches. For players, it places them on a national stage, along with the fact that they do not have to pay college tuition.

Chad and I still talk about his game, competition, and academics. I am here to give motherly advice on life. I try to attend many games as possible. I root for his team, his conference and respect his coaches. I repost stories and photographs on my social media. Other than that, I believe I have shepherded him enough. I am hands off, unless he, or his coaches, request my help. Chad knows what he is doing— most of us find our way in college. I am extremely proud of the man and the player he has become.

If my son, or yours, gets to the professional level, his coach will likely guide him. There are also other professionals at that level who will reach out to him. One of those people may be a sports agent.

Sports Agents

To play professionally in the United States, a player should have a sports agent. For an overseas career, they are helpful but not mandatory.

The best thing I like about agents is that it is unlawful for an agent to give false or misleading information or make false promises. Agents are regulated by the U.S. Federal Trade Commission (FTC)[94] and must also meet the requirements of state licensing agencies and sports leagues. Agents tend to the financial affairs of basketball players. They manage contract negotiations with team leaders and sponsors, as well as recommend financial advisors. For some reason, Tom Cruise's character as Jerry MacGuire, which was based on the real-life of sports agent, Leigh Steinberg, always pops into my mind when I think of them.

Agents work long hours, attend games, help set up housing, and manage public relations for a player. This includes ensuring players conform to any personal conduct clauses in their contracts. Some agents begin their careers as basketball players. Many of them hold a bachelor's and a law degree, which I imagine comes in handy for contract reviews, negotiations, and execution. Agents earn base salaries paid by the players they represent and receive a percentage of players' earnings.

The number one ranked basketball sports agent for contract revenue is Jeff Schwartz. *Forbes* describes him as the "world's foremost basketball agent."[95]

Schwartz is the president and founder of Excel Sports Management. Excel's clients include Russell Westbrook (Utah Jazz), Kevin Love (Cleveland Calivers), Brandon Ingram (New Orleans Pelicans), and Cole Anthony (Orlando Magic).

Eugene Parker, Esq. (1956-2016) was the first Black sports agent and he represented many notable players, including football players Deion Sanders and Emmitt Smith. Parker played for Purdue before being drafted by the San Antonio Spurs in the 1978 NBA draft.

Some of the top sports agent firms include: Creative Artists Agency (CAA), Excel Sports, Priority Sports & Entertainment, Relativity Sports, Lagarde Unlimited, Goodwin Sports Management, BDA Sports Management, ASM Sports, Landmark Sports Agency, Octagon, Athletes First, Wasserman Media Group, WME, and Klutch Sports Group.

If you're curious, you can search for certified agents at nbpa.com (includes FIBA-certified agents) and hoopagents.com. For agents representing the European leagues, visit Eurobasket.com.

Professional Leagues

> *"As coaches, our job is to nudge them in the right direction, but we don't control them. They determine their own fate."*
> Coach Steve Kerr, Golden State Warriors

There are several options for playing professional basketball.

I was intrigued when I learned that many players have carved out their own unique pathways. There is hope for all. Coach Rivera has a saying for his players, #PaveYourPath.

If your son is in college, their head coach and athletic director will help gauge their readiness to go pro. If they are not planning to go to college, they can secure an agent, as well as look to other leagues featured in this chapter.

The National Basketball Association (NBA)

I believe many basketball parents will agree that most young basketball players dream of an NBA career.

The NBA, headquartered in New York City, is the premier basketball league in the world. It was founded on June 6, 1946, after Walter Brown, a former owner of the Boston Garden, produced the idea to host basketball games on the nights when his hockey team was not playing. Brown created the Basketball Association of America, which merged with the National Basketball League, and created the NBA.

The NBA's mission is to "inspire and connect people everywhere through the power of basketball."

The oldest NBA team is the Sacramento Kings.

The NBA, which has over 1,000 employees, does much more than entertain basketball fans worldwide. They also influence pop culture and fashion.

However, what many may not know is that the NBA is a global ambassador of goodwill and philanthropy.

According to the NBA's 2021-2022 Impact Report, they are "committed to taking collective action through the NBA Foundation, National Basketball Social Justice Coalition, the promotion of greater civic engagement, the fostering of economic empowerment, support for Historically Black Colleges and Universities (HBCU), and advocating for greater LGBTQ+ inclusion, as well as gender equity."[96]

Through the NBA Cares, which was created in 2005, volunteers have provided 6.2 million hours of hands-on volunteerism to community organizations and other programs in 40 countries and territories.

Many years ago, I had the privilege of working with the NBA Cares and the New Jersey Nets. I can still recall the day I spent with NBA legend Willis Reed, Jason Kidd, and Byron Scott #4, another one of my favorite Lakers, who was the head coach of the Nets at the time. It was a fun-filled day, and they brought so much joy to the children who attended.

In 2020, the same year as the tragic death of George Floyd, the NBA, in partnership with the NBPA, created the NBA Foundation. Their mission is "To drive economic opportunity in the Black community through employment and career development by funding programs that generate successful transitions from school to meaningful employment for Black youth." To date, the Foundation, led by executive director Greg Taylor, has distributed 165 grants totaling $73 million. It is a part of the Foundation's pledge to distribute $300 million over ten years. Recently, I worked on a team which received over $1 million dollars to provide IT training to young Black men. Worthy grant recipients have included the D.C. Central Kitchen, iMentor, Year Up, and the Campaign Against Hunger.

How Do Prospects Enter the NBA?

One and Done

The concept of "one and done" was created in 2005 when former NBA Commissioner and Attorney David Stern (1942-2020) ruled that players had to be at least 19 years before earning an NBA paycheck. They also must have completed one year of college or one NBA season had passed since they graduated from high school.

Until the 1990s, almost all of the top NBA picks played their full four years in college, including legends Bill Russell, Oscar Robertson, Kareem Abdul-Jabbar, Bill Walton, and Ralph Sampson.[97]

If your son is an extraordinary high school player with the potential to be among the top players in the world, "one and done" may be an option. It seems to be the ideal way for many first-round, number-one draft picks. In the 2022 NBA draft, most prospects were college "one and done" freshmen. The last non-freshman selected as a first-round pick was sophomore Blake Griffin (Los Angeles Clippers) in 2009.

Four first-round picks were seniors: Ochai Agbaji (Kansas/Cleveland Cavaliers), Andrew Nembhard (Gonzaga/Indiana Pacers), (Vince Williams, Jr. (VCU/Memphis Grizzlies), and Tyrese Martin (UCONN/Golden State Warriors).[98]

The NBA and NBPA representatives have discussed the one and done could be over as early as 2024.[99] The draft age would be lowered from 19 to 18 years old, and the high school pipeline to the NBA would reopen. The change will not only help the League recruit new talent but should also present more optimism for future high school players and parents. Commissioner Silver discussed why the change would be good for the League:

> *"I think something has to change. It's clearly not working for the college game. From our standpoint, if the players in that one year of college aren't getting the kind of development we like to see them get coming into the NBA, aren't playing in the NCAA Tournament, aren't competing against top-notch competition, I think we have to take a step back and figure out if we're better off taking those players at a younger age and working on their training and development full-time."*[100]

Declaring for the Draft

Once a college student declares for the draft, he is considered a professional. Although he can return to college to finish his degree, he is no longer eligible to play college basketball.

Getting invited to the draft combine is the door to the draft. Think of it as a job fair for basketball players. Prospects are automatically eligible if they have completed four years of college. If a prospect did not attend college but four years have passed since they attended high school, they can also be considered. A prospect must also pass background and social media checks. The combine allows a prospect to work out for teams before deciding whether to stay in the draft and hire an agent. If a prospect does not get selected for the draft, a team can still sign a recruit on as a free agent and attend an NBA team's training camp.

A thoughtful gift for your son.

Take him to an NBA draft currently held at the Barclay's Center in NYC.
Tickets are less than $100.
You can also purchase an NBA experience where you can meet the draftees or take a picture with the championship trophy.
Visit nbaexperiences.com for more information.

Other Options

Although it is the most spectacular, getting officially drafted is not the only entrance into the NBA.

- **Mitchell Robinson**: Had four offers out of high school. Before he played any college games, Robinson decommitted his freshman year at Western Kentucky (considered a mid-major college). Instead of sitting out a year at another college, he spent the year training for the NBA draft. It turned out to be a smart and strategic move. Robinson was selected by the New York Knicks in the second round, the 36th pick in the 2018 NBA draft. He received a three-year $4.7 million contract. In 2022, he re-signed a four-year $60 million contract to stay with the Knicks.[101]

- **Darius Bazley,** who had 13 offers out of high school, declined to play at Syracuse to go into the G League. He changed his mind and decided to take a year off for training. Bazley then secured a $1 million internship at New Balance. His unconventional path paid off. Bazley, who plays with the Oklahoma City Thunder, was selected in the first round as the 23rd pick in the 2019 NBA draft.[102]

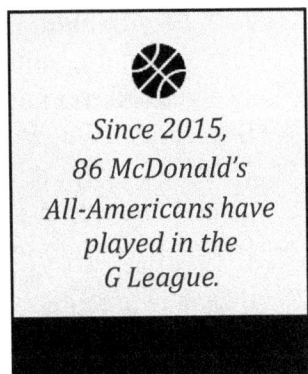

Since 2015, 86 McDonald's All-Americans have played in the G League.

- **NBA Two-Way Contracts** are for players with fewer than four years of experience playing in the NBA who went undrafted (although there are some first and second-round picks on two-way contracts as well). Two-way players are often considered the "16th and 17th men" on a roster. These players are on a retainer; they play on the regular team and for the G League team. They can also be cut at any time and are limited to two years on a two-way contract with the same team. Players earn a flat rate of $449,155 (equal to half the league's minimum salary, which is $1 million for the 2022-2023 season).

- **NBA Exhibit 10 Contract** is another way to get signed to an NBA team. A player can work through a single-season, minimum-salary NBA deal. It is a way for a player to impress a team. Players can earn a bonus of $5,000 to $50,000 if they are waived by the NBA team, sign with a G League team, and stay on for 60 days.

- **NBA Gatorade League (the G League)** In 2017, Gatorade became the first title sponsor of a U.S. pro sports league, and the former Development League (D League) became the G League. The G League is a minor league with 30 teams.

  A player must be 19 years old and one year removed from high school to play (the same as declaring for the NBA draft). NBA G League teams hold open tryouts before each season. You can find information on them at gleague.nba.com under "local tryouts." The Rio Grande Valley Vipers (Houston Rockets) also offer summer training camps for kids 6-13 years old.

- **NBA Professional Pathway Program** is a G League initiative where elite prospects who are not yet eligible for the NBA participate in a one-year development program separate from the traditional G League team. In addition to their salary, which can go up to $500,000 per year, players are afforded basketball development, life skills, mentorship, and a full scholarship to Arizona State. Jalen Green (Houston Rockets) was the first to sign in 2020.

G League president Shareef Abdur-Rahim, who played in the NBA for 12 years, shared in an ESPN interview why the program is important:

> "We have kids leaving the United States — Texas and California and Georgia — to go around the world to play, and our NBA community has to travel there to scout them. The NBA is the best development system in the world, and those players shouldn't have to go somewhere else to develop for a year. They should be in our development system." [103]

Playing Overseas and Worldwide Governing Body

- The **Euroleague** (also known as the Turkish Airlines EuroLeague) is a popular league for American players. According to their website (euroleaguebasketball.net), they "bring the elite of European basketball to all five continents and to the entire sports community..." The Euroleague comprises 18 teams, and salaries range from $150,000 to $5.4 million per year. You can keep up with players all around the world, as well as look up salaries via Eurobasket.com, which covers 435 leagues in 196 countries.

- **The Basketball Africa League** is a joint project between the NBA and the International Basketball Federation (FIBA). It is Africa's "premier" men's basketball league with 12 teams.

- **Canadian Elite Basketball League** (CEBL) - Founded in 2017, the CEBL has ten teams and is the largest pro sports league in Canada.

- **Chinese Basketball Association (CBA)** – The CBA is a 20-team professional league in China. Although international players are limited, many Americans have had lucrative careers in the CBA, including Stephon Marbury, Gilbert Arenas, and Kenyon Martin.

Salaries range from $250K annually to a maximum of $4 million for foreign players.

- **The National Basketball League** (NBL) oversees the leagues in Australia and New Zealand.

- **FIBA: The International Basketball Federation** (also known as The Fédération international de basket-ball amateur) was founded in 1932 and is the world governing body for basketball. Their mission is "To develop and promote the game of basketball, uniting the wider basketball community, which counts more than 450 million players and fans." FIBA organizes the Basketball Champions League (BLC) and international competitions, including the Olympics Basketball Tournaments, FIBA Basketball World Cup, and the FIBA Women's Basketball World Cup.

Other Professional Teams and Leagues

- Playing for the **Harlem Globetrotters** is another professional basketball career option.

The Globetrotters are an iconic American exhibition team. Their basketball home is the Footprint Center in Phoenix, AZ. According to their website, it was founded in 1926 by Abe Saperstein. There is another version that states Tommy Brookins created the team in 1926 in Chicago. The Sports History Network (sporthistorynetwork.com) reports, in an investigative piece, that their founding is "shrouded in mystery." [104]

The Globetrotters continue to entertain basketball fans all around the world "by combining athleticism, theater, and comedy."[105] An annual draft is conducted for prospects who attend a minicamp every August. They also draft "notable figures." In 2022, Issa Rae, Dawn Staley, Shannon Sharpe, J. Cole, Hill Harper, Marlon Taylor, Prince Moss, Evan Clayborne, Darnell Rogers, and Alyssa Naeher were drafted."

There is a form to apply on their website for their travel team which "focuses on showmanship, impressive leaps and dunks, and world-class athleticism in choosing potential future teammates."[106] Website: harlemglobetrotters.com.

- ***Overtime Elite (OTE)*** was launched in 2016 as a social media platform. OTE has grown into a basketball league and a seven-on-seven football league. According to their website, OTE is "a transformative new sports league that offers talented young basketball players a better pathway to becoming professional athletes." OTE teams feature top high school rising juniors, seniors, and post-graduate athletes. Each athlete receives a guaranteed minimum salary of at least $100,000 per year, another $100,000 for college expenses, plus bonuses and equity shares in Overtime. *Forbes* reported in July 2022 that OTE received a $100 million investment from Liberty Media and Winslow Capitol to add women's sports in 2023.[107] Website: overtimeelite.com

- **The HBCU Basketball Association (HBCU BA):** Founded by Kimberly Meadows Clark, the HBCU BA "hopes to broaden professional opportunities for players who attend or attended one of the legendary [HBCU] institutions."[108]

  The inaugural season is set to start in February 2023 through June 2023. The league is for players 18 years and older that are not currently in the NBA or the G League. The HBCU BA also promises that both male and female athletes will "earn equal pay and equal playing time" as a part of their mission. Current sponsors include Spirit Airlines, Cricket Wireless, and BodyArmor. Website: thehbcuba.com

- **The Basketball League (TBL):** Founded in 2017, the TBL's CEO is Evelyn Magley, the first African American woman to own a male professional sports league in the United States.

  Their website notes that TBL is "dedicated to delivering a world-class professional basketball experience to the local community, our fans, and business partners." Players earn between $500 and $5,000 per month. Their 40+ teams are in the following states: Alabama, Arkansas, California, Connecticut, Florida, Indiana, Kentucky, Louisiana, Massachusetts, Michigan, New Jersey, New York, North

Carolina, Ohio, Oklahoma, Oregon, Pennsylvania, South Carolina, Texas, and Washington State. Website: thebasketballleague.net.

- **BIG3**: Launched in 2017, BIG3 is a basketball league founded by Ice Cube and Jeff K. Kwatinetz. Former NBA player Clyde Drexler serves as the Commissioner. According to their website, the BIG3 is "a new, 3-on-3, half-court basketball league that will feature some of the best players to play the game." Website: big3.com.

Final Thoughts on Going Pro

As I have shared, there are many pathways to playing basketball professionally. If you, and your son, think it is a viable option, do not let anyone deter you. Thinking with a business mindset, it comes down to supply and demand.

Professional leagues will continue to have a demand for players, and there will be a need to supply that demand. Why shouldn't you and your son believe he can be one of them?

We know that success in any career is likely earned through hard work. One can also hope for a stew of good luck, good people, and, most of all, God's blessings. Bob Dylan wrote:

"Some people feel the rain, others just get wet."

It is my belief that all young people can reach their dreams, whether in sports, technology, or any other career. Encourage the ones who are putting in the effort.

Tell your son you are proud of him. Work with him. Believe in him. Allow him to dream. Drown out the naysayers and the non-believers.

Becoming a professional basketball player is tough, but so is being one in the youth and college basketball world.

Going pro is my son's dream. Of course, I fully support him and pray that his dreams come true. God has blessed Chad with height and a physical body that is rare. It comes from a unique DNA mixture of Nigerian, Caribbean, South Carolina Geechee, and Irish roots coupled with Brooklyn toughness.

In my final semester at Hunter College, I too worried about becoming a professional journalist. I did not have a job lined up. In one of our monthly meetings, I shared my nervousness with our college's vice president, Dr. Sylvia Fishman, who was one of my "coaches." Dr. Fishman passed away in 2004, but her wisdom has always remained with me.

As I vented to her about my worries, she got tough on me. She sternly told me to focus on graduation and to be proud of my accomplishments as a student editor and leader. She assured me I would land a job and then told me to "stop the theatrics." She produced a handwritten note that she made me read aloud.

> ***"A person should be willing to give up all his tomorrows for one today, so that he doesn't end up wasting all his todays on one tomorrow."***
> *The Alter of Novardik*

Dr. Fishman softly said, "Never forget that, Simone."

Once I pushed my worry aside, in a few months I did land a great job in journalism.

What I gathered from that saying, is that it is best to focus on today while preparing for tomorrow.

One day at a time.

CHAPTER IX

Basketball History & Resources

"Each one should use whatever gift he has received to serve others, faithfully administering God's grace in its various forms."

— 1 Peter 4:10

Young basketball players should know the people in basketball who have made significant contributions to young people. There are countless legends and contributors. I do not purport to know them all. I believe the men highlighted in this chapter are owed a debt of gratitude for their service to young players.

"The fruit our sons eat today were planted by them long ago."

There are also many inspiring movies, books, and podcasts about basketball. I have shared my favorites.

Noteworthy Contributors to Young People in Basketball

- **James Naismith** (1861-1939) was a Canadian-American who invented the game of basketball in 1891 in a gym at the International YMCA Training School (now Springfield College in Springfield, MA). At the time, Naismith was a 31-year-old graduate student whose class was tasked with creating a new indoor activity by Luther Halsey Gulick, the superintendent of physical education. According to Springfield College, Guilick is "renowned as the father of physical education and recreation in the United States."

  After two classmates failed, Naismith decided to try by merging several games into one: American rugby (passing), English rugby (the jump ball), lacrosse (use of a goal), soccer (the shape and size of the ball), and "duck on a rock" which he played as a child in Canada.

  The first hoops were peach baskets nailed to the gymnasium's walls. The first backboards were made to keep fans from blocking shots and interfering with the game.

  A 1939 radio interview is the only recording of Naismith. In it, he describes how the first basketball game ended in a nasty fight. When the game ended, one player had been knocked out, several had black eyes and dislocated shoulders. He then went and added more rules— one of which was not allowing a player to run holding the ball. He said after the new rules were made, they "had a fine sport."

  You can hear the recording on the website of the University of Kansas at ku.edu: Search: *James Naismith's Life and Legacy: Celebrating 150 Years.*

  His two-page *"Originals [13] rules for Basket Ball,"* written on December 21, 1891, and signed by Naismith in 1931, sold in 2010 for $4.3 million at a Sotheby's auction setting a sports memorabilia record.

  You can also learn more about Naismith by visiting The Springfield College Museum, which houses artifacts highlighting his work.

  Naismith also acknowledged,

> *"While the game was invented in Massachusetts, basketball really had its origin in Indiana, which remains the center of the sport."*[109]

Who knew? The residents of Indiana made his invention popular. Go Hoosiers!

- The ***Naismith Memorial Basketball Hall of Fame***, located in Springfield, Massachusetts (the birthplace of basketball), is worth a family trip. Named after James Naismith, the Hall of Fame is an 80,000-square-foot basketball shrine. There you can find information on all inductees on display, fascinating basketball memorabilia, and a gift shop. It is an irrefutable basketball source that preserves the history of basketball.

  Several star-studded events are hosted yearly, and it is also available for private event rentals. Website: hoophall.com.

  The Women's Basketball Hall of Fame is in Knoxville, TN.

- ***Holcombe Rucker*** (1926–1965) created not only the world's most famous basketball tournament in the 1950s, but he also created the slogan, "Each one, Teach one." (See Taking It To The Street(Ball) in Chapter IV to learn more about Rucker).

- ***Bob McCullough*** is a Harlem legend and longtime family friend. McCullough played basketball at Benedict College and, in 1965, was drafted by the former NBA team Cincinnati Royals. Holcombe Rucker was McCullough's mentor. He, along with ***Fred Crawford***, helped continue his dream and kept the Rucker Tournament alive.[110]

- ***Boo Williams*** is one of the premier legends in youth basketball and has coached several professional players, including J.J. Redick, Alonzo Mourning, and Allen Iverson. His bio states, "In 1982, he started a high school AAU basketball program, the Boo Williams Summer League.

  Founded with four teams, there are more than 165 teams and more than 2,000 male and female players."[111]

Williams spearheaded the building of the Boo Williams Complex, a 135,000-square-foot sports complex in Hampton, VA. It is the largest facility of its kind between Washington, D.C. and Greensboro, N.C., and hosts AAU games.

- **Robert Hughes**, the former head coach at Paul Dunbar High School in Fort Worth, TX, was the winningest high school coach from 2003-2010. He is the all-time winning leader in high school basketball, with a record of 1,333 wins.

  Hughes was drafted by the Boston Celtics in 1955 but decided to stay with the Harlem Magicians. He is known for telling his players, "If you can't work hard and put out the best, you probably need to go home to your mama."

- USA Today refers to **John Lucas** as being "widely regarded as one of the foremost authorities for basketball training and development on every level in the world with top college and NBA players flocking to Houston to train in the offseason."[112]

  Lucas played basketball and tennis for the University of Maryland and was the number one NBA draft pick in 1976. He has also served as the head coach for the San Antonio Spurs, Philadelphia 76ers, and Cleveland Cavaliers, as well as the assistant coach and head of player development for the Houston Rockets. I am in awe of his work, one summer, I was tempted to quit my job and move to Houston so Chad could train with him. You can find more information at johnlucasenterprises.com.

- **Morgan Wootten** (1931-2020) was considered the most well-known high school basketball coach. He led the DeMatha Catholic High School team in Maryland for 46 seasons and was hailed as the number one prep school coach of the 20th century. Wootten helped more than 250 student-athletes receive D1 scholarships.

- **Robert J. "Bob" Lanier** (1948-2022) was born in Buffalo, NY, and played at St. Bonaventure (Go Bonnies!). He was the first-round, number 1 pick in the 1970 NBA draft. He went on to become an 8-time All-Star who also served as an NBA global ambassador and spokesperson for the NBA's "Stay in School" program. NBA

The Parent's Section: Outside The Locker Room

Commissioner Adam Silver refers to him as, "one of the most talented centers in the league's history."

Lanier left this earthly realm two weeks before Chad started at his alma mater. I believe his spirit is in St. Bonaventure's Reilly Center's gymnasium. Since the 2022/23 season has started, Chad and other centers on the Bonaventure team have outplayed almost every opposing team's center with a vengeance.

- ***Jack Curran*** (1930-2013) was the former head coach at Archbishop Molloy High School in Queens, NY. He was elected to nine basketball Halls of Fame. Curran was not only a basketball coach but he also won more baseball games than any other high school coach in history. His former basketball players include Kenny Anderson and Kenny Smith.

- ***Tom Konchalski*** (1947-2021) is considered the first basketball scout. In 2013, ESPN made a documentary on his devotion to youth basketball. For over 40 years, Konchalski, who never owned a car, would travel from Maine to West Virginia to publish his newsletter, *High School Basketball Illustrated,* which he told me he still created on a typewriter and was only accessible to coaches via subscription.

During a few other conversations, I would ask his opinion of Chad. He would be brief and say, "He had a good game." "I'll be at the next game." His secrecy made his newsletter "the gospel" for evaluating high school players for college coaches. Konchalski was a special man, and he correctly predicted the success of players such as Kyrie Irving, Bernard King, and Kenny Anderson.

Many players, young and old, gave their condolences on social media after he passed in 2021. Several others ran stories on his passing, including NBA.com,[113] *The Washington Post,* and *Forbes.* Michael "Coach K" Krzyzewski, the former head coach at Duke, said of Konchalski,

> *"There are basketball [G]ods and they send angels to do their work. He was one of them. For Tom, it was never about him. It was about the kids and the game. The game of basketball is better as a result of Tom Konchalski."*[114]

- ***Bob Hurley*** was the head coach at the former St. Anthony High School in Jersey City, NJ. In his 39 years as a coach, he garnered twenty-six state championships and made opportunities for over 150 players to receive D1 scholarships. His son, Bobby Hurley, is the head coach of men's basketball at Arizona State, and his son, Daniel Hurley, is the head coach of men's basketball at the University of Connecticut (UConn).

Other Notable People and Places in Men's Basketball

- ***Ossie Schectman*** (1919-2013) was the first NBA player. Schectman is also credited with making the first basket in the first game ever played, which occurred on November 1, 1946, against the Toronto Huskies in Canada. He went to LIU Brooklyn and played for the New York Knicks.

- ***Earl Lloyd*** (1928-2015) was the first African American to play in an NBA game on October 31, 1950.

- ***Don Barksdale*** (1923-1993) was drafted in 1947 by the Boston Celtics. Barksdale was the first African American player to be named NCAA All-American, the first to play in an NBA All-Star Game, the first to play on an Olympic basketball team, and the first to win an Olympic Gold Medal in basketball.

- ***Nat "Sweetwater" Clifton*** (1922-1990) was the first African American to sign an NBA Contract (1950).

- ***Chuck Cooper*** (1926-1984) was the first African American to be drafted by an NBA team (second round, 13th pick) by the Boston Celtics in 1950.

- ***Harold Hunter, Sr. (1926-2013)*** was also one of the first African Americans to sign a professional contract with the NBA. He was cut from the Washington Capitols during training camp.

- ***Pete Newell (1915-2008)***, born in Vancouver, British Columbia, is considered one of the top American college coaches and was the creator of the Pete Newell Big Man's Camp. Newell was not just a powerhouse on college campuses, he also served as an executive for three NBA clubs and was a General Manager for the Los Angeles Lakers.

- The ***Indiana State Museum***, located in Indianapolis, has a sizable collection of basketball memorabilia in its 500,000+ collection—from Bobby Plump's backboard to Chuck Taylor sneakers.

- ***Marques Haynes*** (1926-2015) of the ***Harlem Globetrotters*** had a 40+ year basketball career. Many consider him to be the greatest dribbler of all time.

- **Meadowlark Lemon** (1932-2015), born in Wilmington, NC, is likely the reason the **Harlem Globetrotters** receive so much love and fanfare worldwide. Lemon is not only considered one of the "greatest" basketball players by Kareem Abdul-Jabbar, but he showed that basketball could be fun for spectators. He toured with the Globetrotters for 22 years and appeared in countless films, television shows, and videos. Lemon was inducted into the Naismith Memorial Hall of Fame in 2003. Michael Jordan referred to him as "a national treasure." He still has an active family foundation at meadowlarkllf.org.

- The History of the **Black Fives** Era – From 1904 until the racial integration of the National Basketball League in the 1940s and the NBA in the 1950s, Black people had their own basketball teams sponsored by churches and social clubs. In 2013, the Black Fives was incorporated by the U.S. Department of Consumer and Regulatory Affairs and is now a public charity. Their website (blackfives.org), sponsored by Puma, includes an online museum and exhibitions about the early days of basketball.

- **The Colored Basketball World's Champion** was a term created by Lester Walton, an editor for the *New York Age*, the most popular Black newspaper at the time. The term was used by sportswriters from 1907-1925 and was created to describe the teams that played during the Black Fives era.

Basketball Associations and Advocacy

- **Baller Moms Canada,** based in Toronto, provides information for basketball and soccer moms of athletes 5-18 years old. Website: ballermom.ca.

- **Jr NBA** is the official youth basketball program of the NBA and the WNBA. Parents can register for free. Under their Parents Initiative, there are parent forums, recommendations, and age-appropriate curriculums. Parents also receive newsletters, information on child safety in sports, basketball basics, and a 15% discount on any order of $50 or more at the NBA store.

  Jr. NBA affiliate teams fall under a membership-based program for existing youth basketball leagues/organizations. Teams can apply to join. Once a member, they can apply for grant funding, obtain discounted uniform offers, and access a national network. Parents can share that information with their son's coach to see if their team can be involved. Website: jrnba.com.

- **Moms Team** is a comprehensive website with information for sports parents. Topics include health & safety, nutrition, and successful parenting from team moms/coaches. Website: momsteam.com.

- **National Association of Police Athletes/Activities League** is an organization "based on the conviction that young people if reached early enough, are more likely to become productive adults and agents of change." There are organizations in many police departments around the country. Police officers serve as coaches, mentors, and tutors. Most are called Police Athletic Leagues (PAL), and there are also Sheriff Activities Leagues (SAL). The organization participates in basketball, soccer and football, and other sports. Website: nationalpal.org.

- **National College Players Association (NCPA):** The NCPA is a nonprofit advocacy association that leads the college athletes' rights movement. NCPA advocacy has made health and safety, Title IX enforcement, and fair compensation several key areas of focus in Congressional hearings. Free membership is open to current and former college students and general supporters. Website: ncpanow.org.

- **National Sports Parents Association (NSPA):** The objective of the NSPA is "to provide parents with a sports road map of the most up-to-date information on technical skills, mental focus techniques, footwork skill development, nutritional secrets, physical conditioning, equipment specifics, and tactical strategies from around the world." Website: nationalsportsparentsassociation.com.

- **UCR Center for Athletes' Rights and Equity (CARE):** Their mission is "to address structural inequalities in sports and to create better more equitable experiences and outcomes for amateur, collegiate, and professional athletes." Website: athletescare.ucr.edu.

- **USA Basketball** was founded in 1974 as the Amateur Basketball Association of the United States of America. USA Basketball is responsible for the "selection and training of the men's and women's national teams that represent the United States in international tournaments." Their comprehensive website provides information on player development and has youth podcasts for coaches. They also advertise a sports mentoring program that provides opportunities for students of color in sports administration. Website: usab.com.

Basketball Informational Websites

The following are sources to find player profiles, basketball statistics, scores, and current news about youth, college, and professional basketball.

- *Athletesinaction.org*: According to their website: "We dream of a day when there are Christ-followers on every team, in every sport, in every nation." They operate from a 250-acre sports complex and retreat center in Ohio.

- *Basketball.realgm.com* – Ryan Hoak leads the "Real GM." Their website states that it is "one of the world's most comprehensive sports sites," and users are offered "all the data and tools required to simulate the experience of a real general manager." Check out the section for high school basketball, which includes forums, news, schools, and awards.

- *Basketball-reference.com/stathead.com* – Their website states that they are "The Most Powerful Research Tools in Sports. Find player, any team, any season, any game, any play." This includes player stats and history in the NBA, ABA, WNBA, and top European competitions. They also have a section entitled "Born on this Day" and "In Memoriam."

- *Bleacherreport.com* – A service of the Turner Broadcasting System (TBS), *The Bleacher Report* state they "capture and unleash the untapped power to deliver visceral, authentic moments at the intersection of sports and culture."

- *ESPN.com* – ESPN (Entertainment and Sports Programming Network) dominates sports coverage. It is owned jointly by The Walt Disney Company and Hearst Communications. ESPN is the leader in providing information on basketball players and the sports industry overall.

- *Maxpreps.com* – MaxPreps, a service of CBS Sports/CBS Interactive, calls itself "America's source for high school sports." **247 Sports** (247sports.com) is also their site, and it allows you to "stay up to date with all the college sports news, recruiting, transfers, and more."

BASKETBALL HISTORY & RESOURCES

- *Moneysmartathlete.com* – The leaders at Money Smart Athlete share, "Currently, there is a lack of an organized global initiative in connection with the financial education of athletes." Their services include, "educating and empowering athletes to make sound financial decisions by cultivating financial literacy as a life skill for athletes of all ages and levels."

- *NSR-Inc.com* – The National Scouting Report, founded in 1980 by Bob Rigney, provides help to college athletes and coaches in the recruiting process. They also share information on how to become a college scout.

- *Reformedsportsproject.com* – Founded by Nick Buonocore, he states, "I started The Reformed Sports Project to provide a platform for coaches and athletes from the highest levels to share their perspective and experiences with parents and kids." On their website, parents can find a podcast, blog, Coaches' Corner, and mental health information for athletes.

- *Sports-reference.com* – If you need sports statistics, Sports Reference is a go-to source. They claim on their site, you can find information on "Every NBA and every WNBA player." They also have a list of every NBA Hall of Famer. Another great resource is that, as a parent, you can find any college coach's win/loss record.

- *Proballers.com* is a great place to look up the stats of college players. They also have a feature to embed a player on any website.

- *Usatodayhss.com* - *USA Today* High School Sports offers a weekly column on the college recruiting process, as well as coverage of high school sports.

THE PARENT'S SECTION: OUTSIDE THE LOCKER ROOM

Twitter Accounts Parents May Find Interesting

- **@AAU_Bingo**: A humorous look at the AAU circuit.
- **@AdamFinkelstein** is the Director of Scouting @247Sports and the College Basketball Insider @CBSSportsHQ.
- **@BabersGree**: Mary Babers-Green is the mother of NBA player Draymond Green. With over 32,000 followers, she was considered the official "NBA Twitter Queen." In 2022, she deactivated her account, but basketball moms need her! I hope she returns.
- **@BallisLife:** With over one million followers, BallisLife is a comprehensive social media site (and website: ballislife.com) for everything basketball. On their app, there is also an option to let players upload their highlight videos.
- **@Daves_joint:** David Cordova is a diligent millennial sports reporter who travels from coast to coast. His Twitter describes Dave's Joint as "A website [davesjoint.net.] dedicated to high school, college, professional and summer league basketball."
- **@HBCU365:** Covers recruiting and sports at Historically Black Colleges and Universities (HBCU).
- **@JBoddenNYC:** Founder of HoopDreams_NYC, Bodden is a sports writer and content creator who has a great handle on the high school basketball circuit.
- **@JonRothstein**: The host of the College Hoops Podcast refers to himself as "College Basketball's Hungriest Insider."
- **@NERRHoops:** New England Recruiting Report (NERR) Hoops.
- **@PaulBiancardi** is the National Recruiting Director for ESPN. He is a former basketball coach and a basketball analyst with noteworthy commentary.
- **@Fullcourtvision**: If you have a son who plays the center position, Reg Butler has probably already found him. Reg is the host of the "Big and Tall Power Hour," which is the only consistent online show devoted to helping basketball's big men.
- **@Rhossi_Carron** oversees U-Sports Group and provides helpful videos to parents and recruits. His insight on youth basketball keeps me intrigued. U-Sports also hosts a Grassroots Summit.

BASKETBALL HISTORY & RESOURCES

- **@Thacoachmike:** Mike Boynton, the Head Basketball Coach at Oklahoma State University, delivers youth basketball commentary.

- **@SFHShoops**: Todd Wolfson, the Head Basketball Coach at St. Francis High School in La Canada Flintridge, CA, has a lot to say to high school parents in a witty but serious way.

- **@Top100Camp:** Created by the National Basketball Players Association (NBPA), the Top100Camp assists elite high school student-athletes with basketball and life skills. Their website (top100camp.com) also features a Top 100 Parent Program.

- **@TweetsbyCoachP**: William Payne creates daily posts about college recruiting with engaging dialogue from parents and coaches.

- **@VerbalCommits and @VerbalCommits2:** With nearly 100,000 followers, Verbal Commits tracks the college commitments of student-athletes.

- **@Wojespn**: With nearly 6 million followers, Adrian Wojnarowski is a well-respected journalist who works as the ESPN Senior NBA Insider. A tweet, retweet, follow, or mention from him is like gold to young basketball players. He also covers breaking news, reports stories, and provides insights about the NBA. Wojnarowski is a graduate of St. Bonaventure (Go Bonnies!) and the author of *The Miracle of St. Anthony: A Season with Coach Bob Hurley.*

Basketball Films, TV Shows & Documentaries

- **Above the Rim** – A sports drama about a high school basketball star in New York City starring Tupac Shakur and Duane Martin.
- **A Kid from Coney Island** – The Netflix description of this film is, "From gifted athlete to professional NBA hooper, Coney Island's Stephon Marbury navigates the pressure, pitfall, and peaks of his basketball journey."
- **Amateur** – A Netflix film starring Michael Rainey, Jr. who gives a brilliant performance. Netflix describes the film as "After he's recruited to an elite prep school, a 14-year-old basketball phenom is confronted by corruption and greed in amateur sports." It is a must-see, 5-star film. Bravo to the award-winning writer and filmmaker, Ryan Koo, who is the Founder and CEO of the website, No Film School.
- **Basketball County: In the Water** – Since 2000, Prince George's County, Maryland, has produced 25 NBA players, including Kevin Durant. This is their story produced by Showtime Networks.
- **Basketball Wives** is a reality show about the lives of professional basketball players' wives, ex-wives, and girlfriends.
- **Black Magic** is a four-hour documentary on ESPN that portrays the on- and off-court struggles of Black basketball players at HBCUs.
- **Blue Chips** is a sports drama film directed by William Friedkin, written by Ron Shelton, starring Louis Gossett, Jr., and Nick Nolte as a college coach trying to recruit a winning team. Actors include former NBA players, Shaquille O'Neal and Anfernee "Penny" Hardaway, with cameos from prominent basketball figures Bob Knight, Rick Pitino, George Raveling, Bob Cousy, Larry Bird, Jerry Tarkanian, Matt Painter, Allan Houston, Dick Vitale, Jim Boeheim, Dan Dakich, and Bob Hurley.
- **Bringing Up Ballers** is a docuseries on Lifetime about the real-life story of entrepreneurial moms whose kids were elite young basketball players in Chicago.
- **Bring Your A Game** - Although not technically a basketball-themed documentary, this 30-minute film produced by Mario Van Peebles, with commentary from Chris Rock, Ice Cube, Spike Lee, Hill Harper,

and Sean Diddy Combs, gives an in-depth look into sports and music careers as options for young Black men.

- **Doin' It In The Park** – An independent documentary by Robert Garcia and Kevin Couliau tells the story of New York City's streetball culture with commentary from Julius "Dr. J" Erving, Kenny Anderson, and streetball legend, Pee Wee Kirkland.
- **Gap Year** – Tells the story of how Darius Bazley made an unconventional path for himself to the NBA by skipping college and the G League to train and intern at New Balance.
- **Glory Road** – A sports drama film, starring Derek Luke and Jon Voight, based upon a true story surrounding the 1966 events leading to the NCAA's first championship team with an all-Black starting lineup.
- **Go, Man, Go!** – This 1954 film tells the story of the Harlem Globetrotters, starring Sidney Poitier and Ruby Dee.
- **Greatest Mixtape Ever!** – A ESPN documentary about streetball in the 1990s. The film is narrated by Jadakiss and features interviews with Fat Joe, Funk Master Flex, Iman Shumpert, Isiah Thomas, Kemba Walker, Lou Williams, Rafer Alston, and Scoop Jackson. A similar documentary is ESPN's **A Streetball Mixtape**, which documents how streetball has influenced the game of basketball and culture.
- **Hardwood** – A documentary short film about Canadian director Hubert Davis' relationship with his father, former Harlem Globetrotters player Mel Davis.
- **He Got Game** – A Spike Lee Joint starring Denzel Washington and NBA Player Ray Allen, among others. Many believe it is based on the life of basketball player Stephon Marbury.
- **High Flying Bird** – A Netflix film about a professional basketball player and his agent who negotiates for him during a NBA lockout.
- **Hoop Dreams** – A documentary about two African American players from Chicago (William Gates and Arthur Agee). The film won the Audience Award for Best Documentary at the 1994 Sundance Film Festival and grossed over $11 million worldwide.

The Parent's Section: Outside The Locker Room

- **Hoosiers** – Nominated for two Oscars, this film stars Gene Hackman as a basketball coach for a small school. It is a film of determination and a real tear-jerker at times. That must be why *Sports Illustrated* and ESPN rated it as "one of the best sports movies."
- **How to Get DI Basketball Offers Fast!!** Jaylen Clark (UCLA Bruins) has created a 30-minute YouTube video that has unfiltered commentary on his experience as a Top 100 recruit. A must-see for all youth basketball players and parents.
- **Hustle** – This Netflix film starring Adam Sandler, Queen Latifah, and Juancho Hernangomez (Toronto Raptors) is must-see. I loved the story and the guest appearances by current NBA players. It also shows how important rankings are to young players.
- **Klutch Academy** – A documentary by the Klutch Sports Group, featuring their charismatic CEO Rich Paul, who prepares six college basketball prospects for professional careers.
- **Like Mike** – A sports comedy, staring Lil' Bow Wow who portrays an orphan who becomes a talented basketball player after finding a pair of Michael Jordan's old sneakers.
- **Love and Basketball** – A top movie classic among Generation Xers that tells the story of a young woman and young man's journey to a professional basketball career played by Sanaa Lathan and Omar Epps. The film also shares the story of an NBA wife (played by Debi Morgan) who battles infidelity from her husband, played by Dennis Haysbert.
- **Moms Got Game** - A television series about the lives of former WNBA basketball star Pamela McGee and her son, NBA player JaVale McGee (Dallas Mavericks).
- **Rise** – The phenomenal biography about Giannis Antetokoumpo, his brothers and family that portrays their lives from Nigeria and Greece to the NBA. It also depicts the involvement of sports agents and how they collaborate with international players and NBA owners.
- **Semi-Pro** – A basketball comedy about a semi-pro basketball team starring Will Ferrell, Woody Harrelson, and Andre 3000.

BASKETBALL HISTORY & RESOURCES

- **Space Jam** – An animated film starring Michael Jordan, Danny DeVito, Bill Murray and Larry Bird, along with a host of NBA players from the 1990s. *Space Jam* was a childhood staple for Millennials. The idea for the film allegedly came from a Nike ad which featured Jordan alongside Bugs Bunny. Chad says, "Every hooper has seen *Space Jam*."

- **Survivor's Remorse** – LeBron James and Maverick Carter, CEO of SpringHill Entertainment, are the executive producers of this Starz network comedy and sports drama. It stars Jesse T. Usher, who portrays a recently drafted NBA player who moves his family to Atlanta. His mother is played by Tichina Arnold, his hilarious sister is played by Erica Ash, comedian Mike Epps plays his uncle and, RonReaco Lee plays his cousin. It is a must-see for basketball moms and siblings!

- **Swagger** - Created by Reggie Rock Bythewood, Swagger is an Apple+ drama television series inspired by Kevin Durant's experience on the AAU circuit. It has quickly become one of my favorites as it depicts a contemporary angle to the world of youth basketball and how a mother, brilliantly performed by Shinelle Azoroh, is connected. Other actors include O'Shea Jackson Jr., Isaiah R. Hill, and Tessa Ferrer.

- **The Fish That Saved Pittsburgh**– A cult classic basketball film made in 1979 which includes an all-star cast staring Julius "Dr.J" Erving. The story is about a basketball team trying to save a city.

- **The Real MVP: The Wanda Durant Story** - The true story of Kevin Durant's mother depicts her struggles and triumphs as she raised her two sons, Kevin and Tony as a young mother in Prince George's County, Maryland. You will need to have tissues handy for the watery eyes.

- **The Way Back** – A movie starring Ben Affleck, whose character portrays a former high school superstar called back to serve as the basketball coach at his former high school. A great family film filled with great life lessons.

Basketball Books

- *After the Shot Drops* by Randy Ribay
- *Basketball for Dummies* by Richard "Digger" Phelps, a former head basketball coach at the University of Notre Dame.
- *Basketball: Its Origin and Development* by James Naismith. Great insight from the man who invented the game of basketball.
- *By the Grace of the Game: The Holocaust, a Basketball Legacy, and an Unprecedented American Dream* by Dan Grunfeld with a foreword by Ray Allen.
- *Cheat Codes for Student Athletes* by Raymond Dale Colston
- *Elevating the Game: Black Men and Basketball* by Nelson George
- *Eleven Rings* by Phil Jackson and Hugh Delehanty
- *From the Bleachers with Love: Advice to Parents with Kids in Sports* by David Epperson, Ph.D., and George A. Selleck, Ph.D.
- *Game*, An Autobiography by Grant Hill
- *How to Watch Basketball Like a Genius* by Nick Greene
- *I am D1: How to Conquer the World of AAU Basketball* by Chris Meadows, M. Ed. with Dr. Jeffrey Shears
- *Life is a Sport: How Basketball Can Help Your Kid Succeed in Life* by Stephanie Rudnick
- *Mamba Mentality*: **How I Play** by Kobe Bryant
- *Mental Toughness for Young Athletes* by Troy Horne and Moses Horne
- *Net Work*: **Training the NBA's Best and Finding the Keys to Greatness** by Rob McClanaghan with a foreword by Stephen Curry.
- *Parent's Guide to Youth Basketball and Beyond: How to Navigate Your Child's Path to College Basketball* by Kevin Cantwell and Pat Alacqua – This book is written entirely from a coach's and recruiter's voice and will give you an inside look at their thought process.
- *Play Present*: **A Mental Skills Training Program for Basketball Players** by Graham Betchart

- *Shoot Your Shot: A Sport-Inspired Guide to Living Your Best Life* by Vernon Brundage, Jr.
- *Snubbed: A Basketball Season of Triumph, Crisis and Despair at St. Bonaventure University* by Brian Toolan
- *Sports Psychology for Basketball,* published by Peak Performance Sports (peaksports.com).
- *The AAU Basketball Bible* by Troy Horne
- *Walk Like You Have Somewhere to Go* by Lucille O'Neal – Highly recommended for basketball mothers.

Basketball Podcasts

- *Clarity for Parents of Athletes* by Gabe Nossier – "Created for parents who are raising athletes with help from stories of former and current professional athletes about their parents and how they were raised."

- *Court-side Moms with Wendy Sparks* – Wendy Sparks, an NBA mom, hosts a show which is "the first of its kind to focus on the mothers of professional basketball players."

  Currently in its second season, her website states, "Being a mom is hard, but being a mom to a professional athlete, that's a whole other level." Her son, Khem Birch, currently plays for the Toronto Raptors.

- *Hoop Heads Podcast* - Covers a wide range of basketball topics, from the grassroots level to the pros, relevant to coaches, players, and parents.

- *The Young Person Basketball Podcast with R.J. Hampton* (Orlando Magic) – An NBA player has conversations with other pro players to discuss what it is like to be a young professional basketball player.

- *Youth Hoops Pod* by Pro Skills Basketball – Their topics are well-rounded and worth a listen for both parents and players.

AUTHOR'S VIDEO CONCLUSION

ABOUT THE AUTHOR

Simone Joye is a writer, award-winning nonprofit executive and charity fundraiser.

Her family's basketball history dates from the 1950s to the present. She has a host of relatives who have played, or are currently playing, at the highest levels in D1 and D2 colleges, the Euroleague, the G League, and the NBA. Her son, Chad Venning, plays at St. Bonaventure University, and her daughter, A'Shey Venning, is an elementary school operations associate and rising film director.

Joye is a graduate of Hunter College and is the author of *Starting and Building an Awesome Nonprofit for a New Generation* and the editor of the suspense thriller, *Private Betrayal* by S.R. Chase.

For her commitment to helping others, Joye has received numerous awards and accolades including:

- *The Certificate of Special Congressional Recognition* from Congressman Hank Johnson and the U.S. House of Representatives.
- *Outstanding Georgia Citizen* - Georgia Secretary of State
- *Humanitarian Award* – Southern Christian Leadership Conference
- *Norman Borlaug Humanitarian Award*/MedAssets
- *John A. Matthews Community Service Award*, the Prince Hall Master Lodge No.99
- *Be Greater Award* from the Atlanta Hawks and SunTrust
- *Thomas C. Wilson Youth Services Award* - NAACP-DeKalb Cty (GA)
- *Woman of the Year* by the Zeta Phi Beta Sorority
- *Outstanding Print Journalist Award* - Hunter College
- *Scholarship Awards* from the New York Association of Black Journalists and the National Association of Black Journalists (NABJ)

BEYOND THE BOOK
WITH SIMONE JOYE

Beyond the Book for Parents and Players (60 minutes -virtual): Personal help for parents and players seeking to improve their youth basketball experience. This Q&A format allows you to ask questions about your process, increase your chances of earning a college basketball scholarship, and obtain recommendations to legitimate basketball experts and services.

Beyond the Book for Coaches/Parents Workshop
(60 minutes-in-person or virtual):
"An ounce of prevention is worth a pound of cure."
This 60-minute workshop (parents meeting) is designed to represent coaches with parents. It shares the coach's vision, alleviates miscommunications, and develops a winning "player first" mindset. At the conclusion, parents will receive a personalized Coach's Policy Handbook detailing the organization's rules and regulations which they sign to fortify their commitment.

Fund Development: (60 minutes-virtual):
Targeted fundraising strategies through grants and sponsorships are provided to senior leadership and board members of youth sports organizations. Learn how to apply and garner additional funding. Includes a written funding research report.

CONTACT
(301) 725-1572
CEO@SIMONEJOYE.COM

IN MEMORY OF

Al Eford, Jr. (1955 – 2022)

"Since the invention of basketball in 1891, very few individuals have ever encapsulated the game in their hearts and soul like Al."

For nearly forty years, my cousin devoted his career to helping countless young basketball players become great men.

Al was born in Harlem and played high school basketball at Long Island Lutheran High School. He was recruited by the Universities of Pennsylvania, Michigan, and Indiana. He committed to the University of Wyoming, where he played from 1974-1977.

Al had a long coaching tenure with the Riverside Hawks, where he coached future professional players Ron Artest III, Lamar Odom, Erick Barkley, and Rafer Alston.

"Coach Al" passed away on November 27, 2022, after a long battle with cancer. Even with failing health into his sixties, he was still on the court helping young men with Team Durant and at several Baltimore high schools. NYCHoops.net wrote a story on his life and passing entitled, *"Beloved Veteran NYC Coach Dies,"* and The Hoop Post shared *"Remembering Al Eford Jr."*

An online sentiment from one of his players, Brandon Day shared the epitome of his life.

"You showed me what it was like to have college scouts come to my high school to watch my games because I only saw that kind of stuff on TV. I had wished I could accomplish that and you made it happen. You introduced me to 5-star camp to show me I can learn the game of basketball though a lot of different lenses. Last but not least you drilled into our heads that life is more than just basketball and even if we became great ball players, you'd be even more proud if became great men."

REFERENCES

Introduction

1 Ellison, James, LaBelle, Patti, Hendryx, Nona F. M., and Wilkie, Nathanial (1991). When You've Been Blessed (Feels like Heaven) [1991] LaBelle, Patti. Burnin' MCA Records.

Chapter I – Parents: The Real MVPs

2 Gleeson, Scott. "Lebron James Pays Tribute to His Mother on Facetime Following Championship: 'I Hope I Continue to Make You Proud'." USA Today, Gannett Satellite Information Network, 12 Oct. 2020,

3 Hodgson, Stephanie. "Lifetime's Bringing up Ballers Cast Member Nikki Dishes It out on the Show and Creating a Successful Family." *RnB*, 3 Feb. 2021, https://rnbmagazine.com/lifetimes-bringing-up-ballers-cast-member-nikki-dishes-it-out-on-the-show-and-creating-a-successful-family/.

4 Lev, Assaf, et al. "No Cutting Corners: The Effect of Parental Involvement on Youth Basketball Players in Israel." Frontiers in Psychology, U.S. National Library of Medicine, 16 Nov. 2020

5 Opinion | In the N.B.A., ZIP Code Matters - the New York Times.

6 'MarcJSpears. "'My Love for My Son Is Underestimated': Why Tee Morant Is out. Front for His Son, Ja Morant." Andscape, 11 May 2022.

7 Das, Shaoni. "The Truth behind Kobe Bryant's Troubled Relationship with His Parents." Goalcast, 22 June 2021.

8 Fighting Spirit:Chad Venning Joins Bonnies Frontcourt Battle , Scott Eddy GoBonnies.com 20 September 2022.

References

9 "The Commercialization of Youth Sports." KU SOE, School of Education and Human Sciences, Department of Health, Sport, and Exercise Sciences, University of Kansas, 23 Aug. 2022.

10 Gregory, Sean. "Kids' Sports Leagues Have Turned into a $15 Billion Industry." Time, Time, 24 Aug. 2017.

11 "IRS Offers Guidance on Recent 529 Education Savings Plan Changes." Internal Revenue Service.

12 15 June 1952, Rocky Mount (NC) Sunday Telegram, "News About Negroes" by R. D. Armstrong, pg. 13, col. 7:

13 Fuemmeler B.F., Anderson C.B., Mâsse L.C. Parent-child relationship of directly measured physical activity. Int. J. Behav. Nutr. Phys. Act. 2011

14 Hellstedt J.C. The coach/parent/athlete relationship. Sport Psychologist. 1987;1:151–160. doi: 10.1123/tsp.1.2.151.

15 Celona, Larry, and Ben Feuerherd. "Dad's Confrontation with Basketball Coach Ends in Double Shooting." New York Post, 25 Dec. 2018.

16 Wire, SI. "Study: Nearly Half of NBA Related to Elite Athlete." *Sports Illustrated*, 25 May 2016

17 "Erik Spoelstra." *Wikipedia*, Wikimedia Foundation, 17 Nov. 2022.

18 Lev, Assaf, et al. "No Cutting Corners: The Effect of Parental Involvement on Youth Basketball Players in Israel." Frontiers in Psychology, U.S. National Library of Medicine, 16 Nov. 2020

19 Martin, Chantz. "Deion Sanders Plans to Lock down Jackson State Players inside Houston Hotel in Wake of Takeoff's Killing." Fox News, FOX News Network, 3 Nov. 2022

20 James Naismith, *Basketball: Its Origin and Development* (New York, 1941; reprinted Lincoln, Nebraska, 1996)

Chapter II – Coaches & Parents Working Together

21 Dr. Jack Welch | Herald-Banner Columnist. *"From The Bleachers: Considering Coaches' Salaries."* Herald, 22 May 2022,

22 National All Sports Virtual Coaches Summit. "*The Role of the Coach in* Recruiting with Paul Biancardi – ESPN." Coaches Insider, 6 Sept. 2022.

23 Dawson, Brett, "How Kenny Payne's Contract for Louisville Men's Basketball Compares with ACC Coaches." Louisville Courier Yahoo! Finance, Yahoo! 26 Sept 2022.

24 Malone, George. "The Highest-Paid College Basketball Coaches in America." —*GOBankingRates*, 3 Apr. 2021.

25 O'Sullivan, John. "*Why Kids Quit Sports.*" *Changing the Game Project*, 17 Sept. 2015, http://changingthegameproject.com/why-kids-quit-sports/.

26 https://en.wikipedia.org/wiki/The_Last_Dance_(miniseries)

27 Lewis, Jade. "What Is NBA Referee Salary in 2022?" CareerExplorer, 13 July 2022.

28 Friday, Jon Solomon |. "Why Youth Sports Refs Are Leaving at Record Rate." Global Sport Matters, 15 Apr. 2022.

Chapter III – The Early Years & High School

29 JULIED. "Youth Basketball: When to Start, What the Rules Are, and How to Stay Safe." MomsTeam,

30 Adam. "Why Kids Should Start Basketball at a Young Age?" Basketball On Point, 14 June 2022.

31 Fenton, Melissa. "Elite Club Sports Teams and the Dramatic Shift in High School Athletics." Grown and Flown, 10 Oct. 2021.

32 Jama, Liban. "Athletes Targeted by Fraud." EY, EY, 3 Mar. 2021.

33 Garland Cooper, Director of Softball NCSA. "Reclassifying: One Year Better but One Year Behind." USA TODAY High School Sports, USA TODAY High School Sports, 8 Mar. 2018.

34 Ben Sherman, SBLive. "NFHS Approves Use of 35-Second Shot Clock Starting with 2022-23 High School Basketball Season." Scorebook Live, 13 May 2021.

REFERENCES

Chapter IV – The Other Seasons: Grassroots & AAU

35 Bobb, Maurice. "John Lucas: From Drug Addict to Life Coach." The Shadow League, 29 May 2017.

36 Smith, Bria. "Nike EYBL Peach Jam Basketball Tournament Brings More Business to North Augusta." WJBF, 18 July 2022.

37 King, Jay. "AAU Basketball, Greed, and Its Effect on the NBA." Bleacher Report, Bleacher Report, 3 Oct. 2017.

38 "Black Student Athlete Summit." Black Student Athlete Summit, https://bsasummit.org/.

39 "Birth of Streetball." New York City Streetball, https://nycstreetball.weebly.com/birth-of-streetball.html.

Chapter V – College Recruitment & Scholarships

40 Kelly Lyell, Coloradoan. "A Real Gamble: Parents of Student-Athletes Spend Thousands on Clubs, Recruiting Services." USA TODAY High School Sports, 4 Feb. 2019.

41 Strauss, Ben. "Colleges' Shift on Four-Year Scholarships Reflects Players' Growing Power." The New York Times, 29 Oct. 2014.

42 NCAA.org. "Division I Board Adopts Changes to Transfer Rules." NCAA.org, 31 Aug. 2022.

43 "Division I Transformation Committee." NCAA.org.

44 Dellenger, Ross. "Mark Emmert's Exit Only the Beginning: More Overhaul Ahead in College Sports." Sports Illustrated, 27 Apr. 2022

45 "Men's College Basketball Teams, Scores, Stats, News, Standings, Rumors." ESPN, ESPN Internet Ventures.

46 Release, Official. "NBA Extends Support across All 107 HBCUS to Advance Opportunities." NBA.com, NBA.com, 21 Oct. 2021.

47 Maas, Jennifer. "Byron Allen's HBCU Go Streamer Strikes CBS Stations Deal for 2022-2023 College Football Season." Variety, 20 Aug. 2022.

48 Bernstein, Dan. "NCAA Nil Roundtable: How People Inside College Sports Would Change Name, Image and Likeness Rules." Sporting News, 18 Sept. 2021.

49 Sayles, Damon. "How Much Do College Coaches Care about Recruiting Camps and the Star System?" Bleacher Report, 2 Oct. 2017.

50 "Ball Screens." MasterClass, https://masterclass.com/classes/stephen-curry-teaches-shooting-ball-handling-and-scoring/chapters/ball-screens.

51 "George Mason HC Kim English Talks College Offers, High School Recruits & More." YouTube, 9 Nov. 2022.

52 Kelly Lyell, Coloradoan. "A Real Gamble: Parents of Student-Athletes Spend Thousands on Clubs, Recruiting Services." USA TODAY High School Sports, 4 Feb. 2019.

Chapter VI – Health & Wellness

53 Iyer, Karthik. "Karthik's Take: Why Do NBA Rookies Keep Getting Hurt?" The Daily Campus, 29 Mar. 2021.

54 Holmes, Baxter. "'These Kids Are Ticking Time Bombs': The Threat of Youth Basketball." ESPN, ESPN Internet Ventures, 11 July 2019.

55 Ben Sherman, SBLive. "NFHS Approves Use of 35-Second Shot Clock Starting with 2022-23 High School Basketball Season." Scorebook Live, 13 May 2021.

56 Holmes, Baxter. "'These Kids Are Ticking Time Bombs': The Threat of Youth Basketball." ESPN, ESPN Internet Ventures, 11 July 2019.

57 Helin, Kurt. "Lebron James Rips AAU Workload: 'AAU Coaches Couldn't Give a Damn about a Kid' - ProBasketballTalk | NBC Sports, 12 Nov. 2019.

58 Youth Basketball Guidelines, https://youthguidelines.nba.com.

59 S.5062 - 116th Congress (2019-2020): College Athletes Bill of Rights, 116th-congress/senate-bill/5062.

60 "Sport Science Institute." NCAA.org.

61 Medcalf, Myron. "Mom: UCLA [Shareef] F O'Neal 'Could've Died' Due to Heart." ESPN, ESPN Internet Ventures, 20 June 2019.

References

62 Neumann, Janice. "Basketball Players May Be at Heightened Risk of Lung Clots." Reuters, Thomson Reuters, 30 Oct. 2015.

63 "Selected Adverse Events Reported after COVID-19 Vaccination." Centers for Disease Control and Prevention, 23 Jan. 2023.

64 "Selected Adverse Events Reported after COVID-19 Vaccination." Centers for Disease Control and Prevention, 23 Jan. 2023.

65 "2019 National Health Interview Survey (NHIS) Data." Centers for Disease Control and Prevention, 14 Dec. 2020.

66 Miller MG;Weiler JM;Baker R;Collins J;D'Alonzo G; "National Athletic Trainers' Association Position Statement: Management of Asthma in Athletes." *Journal of Athletic Training*, U.S. National Library of Medicine.

67 "Stanford Medicine Children's Health." Stanford Medicine Children's Health - Lucile Packard Children's Hospital Stanford.

68 Villanueva, Virgil. "After Sitting out His First Two Seasons, Joel Embiid Found Playing in the NBA Easier than Anticipated." Basketball Network - Your Daily Dose of Basketball, Basketball Network - Your Daily Dose of Basketball, 17 Mar. 2022

69 Sibor, Doug. "A History of NBA Careers Ruined by Injury." Complex, Complex, 17 Apr. 2020.

70 Cannell, JJ, Hollis, BW, Sorenson, MB, Taft, TN, Anderson, JJ. *Athletic performance and vitamin D.* Med Sci Sports Exerc. 2009;41:1102–1110.

71 "Osgood-Schlatter Disease (for Parents) - Nemours Kidshealth." *KidsHealth*, The Nemours Foundation, 1 Jan. 2019.

72 Casa DJ, Stearns RL. *Preventing Sudden Death in Sports & Physical Activity.* Burlington, MA: Jones & Bartlett Publishers; 2017.

73 Rohlin, Melissa. "How Zion Williamson Tuned out the Body Shamers and Came Back Stronger." FOX Sports, 7 Nov. 2022.

74 Love, Kevin. *"Everyone Is Going through Something*: By Kevin Love." *The Players' Tribune*, The Players' Tribune, 28 Feb. 2022.

75 Love, Kevin. *"Everyone Is Going through Something*: By Kevin Love." *The Players' Tribune*, The Players' Tribune, 28 Feb. 2022.

76 Siefert, Kate. "5 NCAA Athletes Die by Suicide since March, Columbus Experts Address Youth Mental Health." WSYX.

77 Zephyr, Alex. "DeMar DeRozan Says Retirement Is the Only Thing That Will Make Him Happy." WFNZ Radio, 29 Sept. 2022.

78 *Samhsa - Substance Abuse and Mental Health Services Administration.* https://samhsa.gov/data/sites/default/files/cbhsq-reports/NSDUHNationalFindingsReport2018/NSDUHNationalFindingsReport2018.pdf.

79 "NCAA Banned Substances." *NCAA.org,*.

80 "Teens." Centers for Disease Control and Prevention, Centers for Disease Control and Prevention, 8 Sept. 2021.

81 "The Contribution of Cannabis Use to Variation in the Incidence of Psychotic Disorder across Europe (EU-Gei): A Multicentre Case-Control Study." The Lancet. Psychiatry, U.S. National Library of Medicine.

82 Morris, Regan. "Fentanyl Overdose: US Teens Fastest Growing Group to Die." BBC News, BBC, 15 Oct. 2022.

83 Silva AM;Santos DA;Matias CN;Minderico CS;Schoeller DA;Sardinha LB; "Total Energy Expenditure Assessment in Elite Junior Basketball Players: A Validation Study Using Doubly Labeled Water." Journal of Strength and Conditioning Research, U.S. National Library of Medicine.

84 "Fast Food Tips for Athletes." *Hospital for Special Surgery*, https://hss.edu/conditions_fast-food-tips-athletes.asp.

85 "Speak up Be Safe for Athletes." *Childhelp*, 7 Feb. 2022.

86 Schuster, Blake. "1 In 4 College Athletes in Survey Say They Were Sexually Abused by Authority Figure." *Bleacher Report*, Bleacher Report, 27 Aug. 2021.

87 "US Center for SafeSport Launches 2020 Athlete Climate Survey." *Team USA*, 6 October 2010.

88 Spoerre, Anna. "'You Forced Evil on ... My Son': Youth Basketball Coach Accused of Abusing Boys for Decades Gets 180 Years in Prison." *The Des Moines Register*, The Des Moines Register, 3 May 2019,

89 Duke, Alan. "Mississippi Basketball Coach Accused of Whipping Players." CNN, Cable News Network, 11 Nov. 2010.

REFERENCES

90 "Protecting Young Victims from Sexual Abuse and Safe Sport Authorization Act of 2017." Wikipedia, Wikimedia Foundation, 13 Oct. 2022.

Chapter VII – Branding & Making Money

91 Tindall, Tommy. "Nil Deals for High School Athletes Can Offer Lessons for Entrepreneurial Teens." MarketWatch, 30 Aug. 2022.

92 Crabtree•8/18/22, Jeremy, and Article written by: Jeremy Crabtree. "NCAA Asking for Help Identifying Nil Pay-for-Play Violations." On3, 18 Aug. 2022.

93 "42-1-18 State Sexual Offender Registry." Georgia Bureau of Investigation.

Chapter VIII – Going Pro

94 Staff, the Premerger Notification Office, and DPIP and CTO Staff. "Sports Agent Responsibility and Trust Act." Federal Trade Commission, 25 July 2016

95 "Profile of Jeff Schwartz." Forbes, 22 Nov. 2022.

96 www.nba.com/." NBA Cares,//cares.nba.com/socialimpactreport/.

97 Jeter, Fred. "'One and Done' Players Large Part of NBA Draft." Richmond Free Press, 25 Nov. 2020.

98 "2022 NBA Draft." Wikipedia, Wikimedia Foundation, 29 Nov. 2022.

99 Lowe, Zach. "Memo: NBA Draft Eligibility Could Shift by 2021." ESPN, ESPN Internet Ventures, 15 June 2018.

100 "Stern Warning: Adam Silver's Threat to Dump One-and-Done Rule Ignores Its Impact on Game's Growth." Sporting News, 17 Sept. 2021.

101 Spotrac.com. "Mitchell Robinson." Spotrac.com,

102 Crain, Nick. "Thunder Forward Darius Bazley's Unique Path to NBA Is Set to Be Featured in a Documentary." Forbes, Forbes Magazine, 22 Oct. 2020,

103 Givony, Jonathan, and Adrian Wojnarowski. "Top High School Player Jalen Green Enters NBA/G League Pathway." ESPN, ESPN Internet Ventures, 16 Apr. 2020.

104 Sports History Network. "The Harlem Globetrotters Very First Game." *Sports History Network*, 18 Dec. 2022

105 "Harlem Globetrotters." *Wikipedia*, Wikimedia Foundation, 19 Dec. 2022.

106 Silverman, Steve. *"Short Stories about Basketball." SportsRec*, 15 Oct. 2019.

107 Young, Jabari. "Liberty Media Leads $100 Million Funding Round for Gen-z Sports Leagues Owner Overtime as Bezos, Morgan Stanley up Stakes." Forbes, Forbes Magazine, 10 Aug. 2022.

108 "News: Historically Black Colleges and Universities Basketball Association Aims to Expand pro Opportunities." HBCU Basketball Association.

Chapter IX – Basketball History & Resources

109 "Indiana Is Basketball History." Macaroni KID Evansville

110 "Bob McCullough (Basketball)." *Wikipedia*, Wikimedia Foundation, 27 Nov. 2022.

111 "History." *Boo Williams Sportsplex*, https://boowilliamssportsplex.com/page/show/1153608-boo-williams.

112 USA TODAY High School Sports. "The Coach John Lucas Blog: The Importance of Player Development." USA TODAY High School Sports, USA TODAY High School Sports, 26 May 2017.

113 Services, From NBA.com News. "Legendary High School Scout Tom Konchalski Dies at 74." NBA.com, 22 Sept. 2022.

114 Feinstein, John. "Perspective | Tom Konchalski Made Basketball Better. the Sport Won't Be the Same without Him." The Washington Post, WP Company, 10 Feb. 2021

NOTES

NOTES

REFERENCES

NOTES

www.ingramcontent.com/pod-product-compliance
Lightning Source LLC
Chambersburg PA
CBHW051049160426
43193CB00010B/1120